The Venture

Angeline A. Fuller

In the interest of creating a more extensive selection of rare historical book reprints, we have chosen to reproduce this title even though it may possibly have occasional imperfections such as missing and blurred pages, missing text, poor pictures, markings, dark backgrounds and other reproduction issues beyond our control. Because this work is culturally important, we have made it available as a part of our commitment to protecting, preserving and promoting the world's literature. Thank you for your understanding.

THE VENTURE.

BY

ANGELINE A. FULLER.

DETROIT, MICH.:
J. N. WILLIAMS, 678 MICHIGAN AVENUE.
1883.

COPYRIGHT, 1883,
BY
ANGELINE A. FULLER.

TO THE READER.

Some of the following poems were composed during seasons of eye trouble, so severe that blindness seemed inevitable, and were carried in memory until a respite permitted their commitment to paper; others were produced on very short notice, in response to official request, privately made, or were arranged at leisure, in obedience to public vote, for assemblages of the Deaf and Dumb, a class whose position and experience is largely more prosy than poetical. These, with others composed under less embarassing circumstances, are now submitted to the reading public, with much regret for all imperfections, and an earnest wish that, despite defects, they may aid in furthering the educational interests of the several classes mentioned in some of them.

A. A. F.

August, 1883.

CONTENTS.

POEMS OF THE DEAF AND DUMB.

Scenes in the History of the Deaf and Dumb,	9
Commemorative,	27
The Deaf-Mute Alumni Reunion,	34
To Whom is Honor Due?	39
Opening Hymn for a Deaf-Mute Convention,	42
Closing Hymn For Same,	43
Acrostic Verses,	45
To a Deaf-Mute Foreigner,	46
To a Hebrew Deaf Mute,	48
Hymn for the Unveiling of a Memorial Tablet,	51
Hymn for the Dedication of a Chapel,	55
To a Deaf-Mute Lady,	56
The March of Progress.	59
The Blind Deaf-Mute,	65
A Strange Half-Century,	67
A Challenge,	71

TEMPERANCE POEMS.

The Whisky-Jug's Revelation,	75
The Pleasant Glass.	75
A Plea,	77
Help the Drunkard to Reform,	78
For God and Humanity,	80

THE VENTURE.

LOCAL POEMS.

PARENTAL LAMENT ON THE DEATH OF TWIN BOYS,	86
OUR FRIEND,	88
IN REMEMBRANCE,	89
THE EARLY DEAD,	92
SUGGESTIONS,	93
PARENTS' TREASURES,	94
THE DEAD MOTHER,	95
TO MOTHERS,	96
ON THE DEATH OF A CHILD,	97
A LESSON FROM FLOWERS,	98
THE OLD GRAVE DIGGER,	101

SONGS AND HYMNS.

MUSIC ALL AROUND US,	104
A CENTENNIAL HYMN,	105
TO-DAY AND TOMORROW,	108
GOD IS GOOD AND GOD IS LOVE,	109
THE STILLING OF THE TEMPEST,	110
A SONG OF EXULTATION,	111
A REQUEST,	113
A THANKSGIVING HYMN,	114
A DOLLAR OR TWO,	115
COUNT THE COST,	117
WHEN WE FORGIVE,	119
LAND AHEAD,	120
BEAR AND FORBEAR,	121
TRY TO BE HAPPY,	122
WE SHALL MEET AGAIN,	124
TRUTH SHALL TRIUMPH,	126
LIGHTS ALONG THE SHORE,	127
THE AGED CHRISTIAN'S TESTIMONY,	129
GOD AND OURSELVES,	130

6   THE VENTURE.

A Wedding Song,   - - - - -   132
Make Flowers Your Friends,   - - - 133
Reflections on Reading the Forty-Sixth Psalm, 134
We Need Not Sit With Folded Hands,   - 135
Here and There,   - - - - - 137
Trust in God Always,   - - - - 138
The Will of God,   - - - - - 139
A Song Suggested by a Song,   - - 141
Nothing is Lost,   - - - - - 142
The Voyage of Life,   - - - - 145
Sweet Memory Bells.   - - - 146
Not Forever,   - - - - - 148
Ask Me Not to Drink,   - - - - 149
A Song for the " Make Home Happy" Army,   - 151
Love and Flowers,   - - - - 153
The First Alarm,   - - - - 155
The Conflagration,   - - - - 156

MISCELLANEOUS POEMS.

The Worth of Prayer,   - - -   116
God's Patience and God's People,   - - 169
A Story and a Sermon,   - - -   174
Woman's Mission and Woman's Work,   - 179
The Menagerie,   - - - -   182
Wonderings,   - - - -   183
City Trees,   - - - -   184
Labor and Capital,   - - -   186
Natal Bells,   - - - -   187
A Bit Of Blank Verse,   - - - 191
The Copy,   - - - -   193
The One Name,   - - -   195
A Protest,   - - - -   198
Friendship,   - - - -   199

THE VENTURE.

7

The Value of a Soul,	200
A Proof of Immortality,	2 1
Finished Work,	202
A Soliloquy,	203
What I Would Do,	206
When I Shall Be Satisfied,	209
Bring Flowers,	210
Good and Better,	212
A Little While,	213
Lines for a Young Lady's Album,	215
Counsel for the Troubled,	216
Life is Like the Weather,	217
No Adverse Change Beyond the Grave,	220
True Rest,	221
Thanksgiving Lines,	222
The Bible,	223
Where is Cliffie ?	224
To a New-Born Infant.	228.
To Mary on Her Wedding Day.	229
After the Wedding,	231

POEMS OF THE DEAF AND DUMB.

SCENES IN THE HISTORY OF THE DEAF AND DUMB.

SCENE FIRST.

Behold a miracle! a bush on fire,
    Burning intensely, burning unconsumed,
Note how the flames rise higher and yet higher,
    And all the air around is high perfumed,
With odors richer far than any flower
    Exhales at day's first dawning, when the Sun
Drinks up the dew-drops and goes forth in power,
    His daily journey leisurely to run,
To carry from the land of song and star
    Brightness and warmth into the west afar. ·

Note further that each wave of perfumed light
    Shimmers and shines as tho' the sun and moon
And all the stars of heaven, most fair and bright
    With all their force of midnight and of noon,
Were multiplied ten thousand thousand times,
    And then ten thousand times ten thousand more,
Until the number aggregates or climbs
    Past computation's limit, mete or score;

THE VENTURE.

Aye, multiplied so brightly that it seems
　Earth's every jewel in one casket gleams.

Well may the air be sweet, well may is shine
　With wondrous radiance, such as was not seen
Ever before, for power we know DIVINE
　Has touched that bush, erewhile so low, so mean,
A common thing, from which each passing brute
　Might browse at pleasure, or by well-aimed blow
Break, nevermore to leaf or bloom or fruit,
　Or thrive beneath the sun's most genial glow,
A bush to be, by any strong man doomed,
　Uprooted, or by common fire consumed.

And see, near this vast.pile of earth and rock
　Known as Mount Horeb, Moses wends his way
Intent upon the pasture of his flock,
　· Intent on keeping evil beast at bay,
Thinking, perchance, of Egypt and the sin
　Of sore oppression he had witnessed there,
Until his soul revolted, and from kin
　He fled, unable more to see or bear,
Fled all alone, in horror and in grief,
　To find with strangers comfort and relief.

Behold his wonder when at first the sight
　So wholly marv'lous, so unparalled,

THE VENTURE.

11

That it would fill a common soul with fright,
  And even him in speechless wonder held
For a brief while, then shaking off all fear,
  Of harm or danger, he right bravely cries,
"Not burnt, strange, very strange, I will draw near
  To see this fire which flickers not nor dies,
But blazes on, surpassing everything
  Of which historians talk or poets sing."

But harken now, for scarcely has his word
  Of firm decision echoed on the air,
Or his broad breast, within so deeply stirred,
  Drawn breath, more of the thrilling sight to bear,
When from the bush there emanates a sound,
  A·voice that thrills him to his being's core,
And bends his soul in homage more profound
  Than any voice had ever done before,
As it commanded, " Nay, do not draw near,
  Take off thy shoes, the ground is holy here."

Having responded promptly to his name
  In the brave words of Abraham, "Here am I,"
And bared his feet before the curious flame
  Which while it rose so brilliantly, so high,
Made the whole plain a consecrated place
  Henceforth, forevermore, while time endures,
A spot historian's pen would sometimes trace,

THE VENTURE.

And venturous trav'lers visit in their tours,
A spot to prove till earth and time shall end
That our Creator also is our friend.

Fitting it was the astonished man should hide
His face in awe and listen in a maze
Of humble, solemn joy that he, denied
Awhile the right to walk earth's peopled ways,
Might in the lonely desert meet his Lord,
And learn from His own lips that He gave heed
To all His children's wrongs, and would accord
Judgment to their oppressors, and would lead
Them forth in triumph to a better land,
Where peace and plenty smile on every hand.

'Twas further fitting that he should reply:
"I hear Thy words, and I would gladly go
Unto Thy people, who in anguish cry,
Yea, I to them Thy promises would show,
But who am I that I should be so blest,
So honored? Thou hast others fitter far
To lead Thy children to their longed-for rest,
Send them to be a guide, a morning star,
To those to whom Thy pledge was long since given
Of Thy best favors granted this side Heaven.

"Yea, I would gladly go, but much I fear
That tho' they long have prayed, are praying now,

THE VENTURE. 13

For a deliverer, or for hope to cheer
   Their hearts, until it please Thee to allow
Their servitude so very long and great
   Entirely and forevermore to cease,
And lead them forth unto their own estate,
   Their promised land of liberty and peace,
Me for their leader they will not receive,
   Nor that Thou sendest me at all believe."

Quickly the Lord whose glory made the place
   So wonderful, made answer: "Do not fear
To do my bidding, I will give thee grace
   For all the way that seems so long and drear.
Haste, bravely haste upon thine honored way,
   Bid the proud tyrant set my people free,
Go without fear of evil night or day,
   For I—certainly I—will go with thee,
To end the long, dark night of cruel woe,
   And to their rest my chosen people show."

Meekly again the favored man replied:
   "I am not eloquent, but slow of speech,
Is there no other better qualified
   Thy chosen people to lead forth and teach?
I have no lack of love for Thine nor Thee,
   But he should have the power quickly to sway
The people's minds who dares a guide to be,

THE VENTURE.

Or Thy commands before them seeks to lay;
And since my speech is poor, my tongue is slow,
    Choose a more fitting guide, and bid him go."

Brighter, far brighter then, glowed the strange fire,
    Shimmered more grandly, every twig and leaf—
Higher the flames rose upward, and yet higher;
    A pause ensued—a silence deep, but brief—
And then the Lord by questions made reply:
    "Who made man's mouth? who made the deaf
        and dumb?
Say, did not I, the Lord? and cannot I
    In any time of need bid words to come?
Fear not, for surely I will go with thee,
    I, the I AM, thy help, thy guide will be.

"But since thou art so diffident, so meek,
    Behold thy brother, Aaron, he shall be
To thee a mouth, and through him thou shalt speak
    Whatever I communicate to thee.
Fear neither king nor people, Lo! the rod
    Thou holdest now, and even thine own hand
Shall henceforth be a sign that I, the God
    Of Abraham, Isaac, Jacob, all, command,
Anoint, appoint and full commission thee
    To lead my captives forth to liberty.

THE VENTURE.

SCENE SECOND.

Right well the Promiser His promise kept,
    And with wise words in every hour of need,
Filled each old prophet's mouth, and Israel slept
    Or waked or journeyed, as His word decreed,
Until at last they gained the promised land,
    And safely dwelt, blessing and being blest,
Till, seeing thev to evil gave a hand,
    Affliction entered in, their faith to test,
And teach that God is ever watching near,
    And notes all lack of love or trust or fear.

Then when they cried for help, wise prophets came,
    Telling them of a time, a happy day,
When by repentance they again could claim
    Much they possessed before they went astray,
Saying the lame should sometime nimbly leap,
    The blind should see with strong and perfect eyes,
The *deaf* hear plainly, and joy yet more deep,
    The *dumb*, no longer dumb, return replies,
And every age should know and should declare,
    God for the suffering has a special care.

And while the years went by, the wondrous years,
    Working their changes great and manifold,
Men nursed high hopes, or sadly talked of fears,

THE VENTURE.

Prayed, toiled and strove for bread, for land and
    gold,
And as their fancy or their means decreed,
    They builded temples in which Science, Art,
Religion, Learning, each could garner seed,
    Of which all devotees could take a part,
And carry forth to strew with generous hand,
    Broadcast, to bless and beautify the land.

Aye, more, they builded Homes, wherein the lame,
    The sick, the weak, could find a place of rest,
When those who were their friends only in name,
    Forsook them, left them helpless and distressed;
Homes, into which the suffering ones could go,
    Until the storm of trouble should pass by,
Or they could drink their mingled cup of woe,
    And calmly, quietly lie down to die.
Aye, for all such every enlightened age
    Left a fair record upon historic page.

But tho' the Lord so plainly had declared
    That He, himself had made the deaf and dumb,
And had His word of honor pledged, He cared
    For each, for all of them, and gave them some
Portion and share and interest due, and claim,
    In every right or privilege of the age,
In which they lived, rights dear even in name,

THE VENTURE. 17

Alike to the uncultured and the sage—
Aye, gave them of all these a liberal share,
And cared for them with loving father care.

They were passed by, neglected, doomed to scorn,
Considered brainless, soulless, useless things,
Men even cursed the house where *such* were born,
And wounded them with worse than scorpion
stings;
Grudged them their food, even grudged them light
and air,
And took their life, without regret or shame,
As if their cry for help—their dying prayer
For justice could not—would not—have a claim
In Heaven's high courts, as if the Lord had not
Vowed care for them, or had his vow forgot.

SCENE THIRD.

Haste with me now across the bridge that spans
The gulf of centuries and with me behold
Another miracle, angelic bands
Filling the eastern horizon, their harps of gold
Echoing sweetest music, and they sing
A song ne'er heard by sin-marked men before—
O, blessed song—earth has at last a King—
"Peace and good will!" Hate, give thy warfare
oe'r;

THE VENTURE.

Man need no longer live to sin a slave—
  IMMANUAL comes to mediate and save.

Proper it was, a new, a brilliant star
  Should rise upon that blessed, blessed morn—
Rise to proclaim to earth both near and far,
  The glorious tidings that at last was born
The true Messiah, who would break the night—
  The long, dark night of fear which sin had wrought,
Bring immortality and Heaven to light,
  By pure, redeeming love, passing all thought,
In measure so immense, no word but so
  Its height nor depth nor length nor breadth can
    show.

A king who comes in pride and pomp to reign
  May look unpityingly on others' grief,
And leave the sufferers to endure their pain
  Till in death's slumbers they can find relief;
But He, the King of Glory, could not go
  Past suffering thus, His mission was to heal
Whom sin had wounded, and by deeds to show
  Where'er He went since He might not conceal
That in the form of weak humanity
  He held the power of true divinity.

THE VENTURE. 19

Therefore he helped the weak—the hungry fed,—
　Let palsied captives from their bondage go—
He healed the sick—called back to life the dead,
　And bade the mourners' tears no longer flow;
He touched blind eyes, and lo! they clearly see;
　He said *Ephphatha* to the lips long dumb,
Applied to silent ears the mystic key
　Of firm command, and bade sweet echoes come,
Then left the happy throngs their joy to tell
　In grateful praise—"He doeth all things well."

O, favored eyes, that opening to the light
　Looked first upon their Saviour; doubly dear,
O, favored ears, that waking from a night
　Of utter silence, first of sounds could hear
The Master's voice, and with the lips long dumb
　Speak first to Him, and thank Him for His love,
That matchless love, which prompted Him to come
　From all the glory of His home above
To take from death its sting, the grave its gloom,
　And save the sinful from their righteous doom.

SCENE FOURTH.

Again haste with me o'er the bridge of time,
　See, we stand now upon our native soil;
It is the hour for vesper bells to chime,

THE VENTURE.

The hour when men can rest awhile from toil,
When children love on grassy plats to play,
　See, there a group is busy at a game;
And there, apart from them a little way,
　Stands one who will not answer to her name,
However loudly they may bid her come,
　For she, alas! is *deaf—is deaf and dumb!*

Has God no pity for the stricken child?
　Does He not care that she is so alone?
Will He not heed her wish, her anxious prayer
　Which she can utter only in a moan?
O, question not, O, question not—He cares,
　He loves the stricken one, and even now
Counts over all her tears and voiceless prayers
　· For a deliverer, let us meekly bow,
Our heads in reverent awe and drop a tear
　Of thankful joy that help at last is near.

She is no common-fated, short-lived one,
　No pretty picture upon which to gaze
A little while, then toss aside or shun
　For grander things; where'er her pathway lays
Her name in history's page henceforth will fill
　An honored place, as sure as Justice weighs
True merit.   Doubt and fear be still, be still.
　Though nothing now the embryo fact betrays,

THE VENTURE.

A grateful, happy girl is waiting here,
   A woman famous for all time is near.

And help is coming, tho' she knows it not,
   Near by a student, weary with his book,
Lays it aside and saunters to the spot,
   Awhile upon the merry group to look ;
And now his eye, his Heaven-directed eye,
   Rests on the silent, isolated one,
Look! hark! he heaves a sympathizing sigh,
   And questions earnestly—"Can naught be done
To set her captive thoughts and feelings free
   And give her mind its natural liberty?"

Surely an angel must have told the child
   He was no common man for her to fear;
Look, she upon his first advance has smiled,
   And shakes her head, meaning, "I can not hear,"
Alas, poor child ; others can say the same,
   Like you, to Heaven for help they long have cried,
And God at last acknowledges their claim,
   And sets the door of mercy open wide ;
But he who longs to teach you first must turn
   To sunny France, a method there to learn.

For there the Abbe de l'Eppe waits
   To teach by graceful movements of the hands

22 *THE VENTURE.*

A way which will, despite each one who prates
  Against it, break effectually the bands
Which have so long held dormant precious powers,
  And doomed full many a noble heart and mind
To idle days, to lonely wretched hours,
  To *ignorance* and all its ills combined,
Waits now, surrounded by a little group,
  The heralds of a vast, exultant troop.

O, blessed, truly blessed, are the hours
  When looking down upon His suffering ones,
God notes their sorrows and their fettered powers,
  Notes how against them time's strong current runs,
Notes till His father heart can bear no more,
  And cries "Enough," and bids deliverance speed
To compass land and sea, nor once give o'er
  Their searching for relief till they are freed
Who cry for help. Such hours are highly blest
  And are of gratitude the constant test.

SCENE FIFTH.

Love is a wondrous leveller indeed;
  The old and young turn twins at its command;
And aliens, at any time, by it decreed,
  Though ears be deaf, and lips be wholly dumb,
Eyes say in tones most sweetly eloquent,

THE VENTURE.

"Fear not, sweet heart, for I will surely come,
Yes we, God willing, will clasp hands again;
   A little while our paths must lie apart,
And till I come, good-bye, fear not, sweet heart."

And though the absence be prolonged for years,
   The kind "God bless you, we again shall meet!"
The anxious, waiting heart sustains and cheers,
   While faith and hope the assuring words repeat,
And fancy, at its pleasure, gaily builds
   Air-castles most magnificiently grand;
Or fond anticipation brightly gilds
   The blessed sometime, when they two shall stand
Together, who, though bound in mind and heart
   By sympathy, awhile must walk apart.

Surely, O, surely, many an angel band
   Hovered about the honored ship that bore
That noble student from his native land
   On his grand mission; surely, too, before,
Aye, with, and after him, God's blessing went;
   And he was kindly guided, day by day,
Favored and prospered, and was duly sent
   Proudly rejoicing on his homeward way,
Bringing a brother helper, 'round whose name
   Justice would sometime twine a wreath of fame.

THE VENTURE.

And just as surely angels hovered near
  That stricken girl, whose isolated state
Challenged that good man's pity, till all fear
  Of danger or of failure, small or great,
Was cast aside, and very often they
  Fed her with hopes—sweet manna of the soul—
Or showed her pictures of that happy day
  When from her life the heavy cross should roll
And she, with fervent, grateful joy elate
  Could promise others freedom yet more great.

SCENE SIXTH.

A ship is slowly sailing into port,
  Fire a salute, let all the land be glad,
Proclaim a gala day of rest and sport,
  Sing thankful songs till not a heart is sad,
Call that poor stricken girl, a maiden now,
  Bid her with grateful kiss of welcome haste
To meet him; bid her make a solemn vow
  Ever to keep his name in memory traced;
Ever to honor him who holds a key
  That soon will set her captive senses free.

Nor hers alone—give God his dues of praise,
  His mercy is not narrow in its scope,
He sets no favored few near joy's warm blaze
  Leaving the many in cold gloom to grope,

THE VENTURE. 25

He hears, He heeds each dumb child's eager prayer,
    And from their lonely, isolated wolds
Will in His own good time, with loving care,
    Gather them into safe and happy folds,
Where signs will picture or will echo sound,
    And break their silence, partial or profound.

O, blessed work, to break the prisoner's chains!
    O, happy task, to give the hungry food!
O, joy untold, to ease the sufferer's pains!
    Or see that rugged paths with flowers are strewed,
And all this blessedness was theirs who gave
    Sound to the deaf and language to the dumb;
Who told them of the Christ that came to save,
    And made them heirs of happiness to come,
This was their angel work, though hard and slow,
    And challenges respect from friend and foe.

Write, proudly write their names, GALLAUDET,
        CLERC;
    Paint them in letters of the richest gold,
Carve them in marble, mention them in verse,
    Of grandest measure, and have often told
In prose most eloquent, how they have wrought
    Emancipation from a bondage dire,
Have given to Heaven-created will and thought

THE VENTURE.

Power to reach outward, onward and aspire,
With hopes of realization, to great heights
Of all that here ennobles or delights.

Call them philanthropists or call them friends,
    But love and honor them forevermore,
And long as vapors rise or dew descends
    · Hold blest the day they stepped upon our shore.
The ship they came in perished long ago,
    And they long since were summoned from the
      field
Wherein they toiled so faithfully to sow
    Seed that each year returns more bounteous yield,
And grateful reapers now throughout the land
    Gather the harvest and pronounce it *grand!*

Gather, then look with hopeful hearts away
    Toward the future, because teachers wait
In phalanx deep, and deepening every day,
    E'en to the borders of our mighty State;
Brave men, whose names 'tis honor to repeat;
    Fair women, wise in love's mysterious lore;
All, all great hearts, whom, though they never meet,
    They feel are friends, true to the inmost core,
Whose plea, whose boast, throughout all time to come,
    Shall rightly be, "We taught the deaf and dumb."

THE VENTURE. 27

COMMEMORATIVE.

On the anniversary of the founding of the first school for the Deaf and Dumb in America. Arranged for the celebration of the ninety-third birthday of the founder, the Rev. Thomas Hopkins Gallaudet, Friday, December 10, 1880.

The years, the years, the wonder-freighted years,
  How fast they fly upon their silent way!
Bearing with them alike our hopes and fears,
  And all that makes the story of each day;
Bearing all to that sea without a shore,
  That circle, which, because it has no end,
We call Eternity, and evermore,
  By varying paths, our way around it wend.

Behold what monuments the years have built,
  Not in the form of pyramids alone;
Not in the shape of brass nor bronze high gilt,
  Nor solid gold, nor marble, granite, stone,
Piled up in useless grandeur here and there,
  As man decrees, throughout the sea-girt land,
To please our whimsey fancies and declare
  The cunning skill of his own brain and hand.

Not in the form of tombs, to tell us where
  Rest those who have achieved some proud success,
Those who are strong to venture, do or dare,
  Or suffer, others' sufferings to redress;

THE VENTURE.

Not in such forms time's noblest work appears,
 For soon, full soon, such crumble and decay,
And by the years, the wonder-working years,
 Are ruined, swept entirely away.

But in the far more glorious, lasting form
 Of homes whereinto each poor, moaning one
Whom fate sends forth to wander in the storm
 Of bleak adversity, whom proud souls shun,
The maimed, the sick, demented, blind and deaf,
 The idiotic even—all assured
That they shall find some measure of relief,
 Be cheered, be taught, relieved, or wholly cured.

Such are the grandest monuments of Time,
 Though very plain or homely they may be,
And each one hallows every inch of ground
 Whereon it stands—and to it proudly flee
As to a Mecca, many a grateful heart,
 That it with pilgrim reverence may pay
Its tithes, its homage true, and then depart
 Stronger, to press upon its rugged way.

And every year which sees such structures rise
 And open to each burdened, suffering heart,
Which sees them nursed, or healed, or kindly cheered,
 Or taught to act in life a worthy part,

THE VENTURE.

Is a rare golden link in Time's vast chain,
　Firm welded, which shall glitter evermore,
Glitter when we are done with grief and pain,
　And stand triumphant on the spirit shore.

And they who plan these monumental piles
　And labor others' sufferings to redress,
Labor undaunted long as heaven smiles,
　To make the sum of earth's great misery less,
Are kings and queens, though never robe nor crown
　Nor sceptre shall be given them here below,
Their throne is grateful hearts, their diadem
　The joy which but the self-forgetting know.

This, but as preface, ye who meet to-day
　In one of these grand monumental homes,
Whose history, were it fully traced, would lay
　Not in mere volumes, but in costly tomes,
Be more than glad for what the years have wrought,
　Be more than pleased for what your eyes behold,
Be jubilant, exultant, strange the thought,
　Yet these plain walls the very earth enfold.

Enfold and influence, silently, yet sure
　As shines the sun by day, the moon by night,
As gleam the stars, the wonder-waking stars,
　In constellations gloriously bright;

THE VENTURE.

Influences as does a mother true,
 Through memory, her child, her wandering child,
Whom if she did not with fond love pursue,
 Might soon be ruined, lost or sin-defiled.

Do any doubt? Of late to me there came
 Hoar-headed, wise, benignant, loyal, true,
MEN who reflect high honor on the name
 Of that blest mental mother, who can do
Right—though they in the doing stand alone,
 Right—though the thoughtless sneer and laud the
  wrong,
Right—sure that while to God all things are known
 They are themselves an host—a mighty throng.

They came to me, not knowing I would heed
 Their coming much, or ever sing their praise,
 Not conscious that the words they dropped were
  seed,
Which would take root, and bear in after days
 Blossoms of earnest thought, and purpose firm,
Wherein my mind and heart, and as is meet,
 Would make their manes, to me, in proper term,
"Incense," forever precious, fresh and sweet.

And they are but a few among the host,
 Of noble men and women, who this hour

THE VENTURE.

Standing on life's fair verge, can proudly boast
  They saw the bud of what is now the flower,
Trod those dear halls as children, ignorant, weak,
  As trembling prisoners, without power to tell
Whence they had come, or whither they would go,
  When time had broken silence' horrid spell.

Trod them as youths, emancipated, saved,
  From such a fate as would make angels weep,
When thinking on it; trod with senses laved
  Not only in the founts which wise men keep
Open to all; but at that freer fount
  Of spiritual knowledge—by the light
Of which we upward from earth's darkness mount,
  And cross in happy triumph death's cold tide.

Trod them as heralds of a growing class
  Who should throughout all time excite the cry—
"What hath God wrought?" How doth he kindly pass
Mercy around, when voiceless sufferers cry,
  How doth he love his children and declare
His love by blessing with impartial hand,
  By making man his agent and his heir,
And honoring him in every age and land.

A class that should pursue earth's winding ways
  As artists, scholars, winning wealth and fame,

THE VENTURE.

As noble laborers, anxious to bequeath
　To their descendants an unsullied name,
That grandest legacy which man can leave
　His heirs or country, when at last he lies
Cold in the arms of death, and fond hearts grieve,
　Venting their sorrow by their tears and sighs.

This theme is grand, so grand I long to dip
　My pen in lurid fire, thereby to trace
More perfectly the joy-inspiring scenes
　Which enter in and cluster round this place,
This anniversary day, lo! angels come
　To hover near and sing triumphal songs
Of praise to him who made the deaf and dumb,
　And unto whom our loftiest praise belongs.

Let the warm-hearted South and generous East
　Clasp hands to-day in kind, fraternal love,
The pioneers—the fathers—let them come
　In spirit, from their blessed home above,
Come to this honored Mother, who has borne
　So many mental offspring—children who
But for their mutual love perchance had worn
　The heaviest shackles life's whole journey through,

Come, and with her, and all who hold her dear,
　Rejoice, exult, that many, O, many a child

THE VENTURE. 33

Who once seemed doomed to live in stupid fear
  And die in ignorance, all sin-defiled,
Is now a happy soul, fully prepared
  To act in life a worthy, noble part,
And go whene'er its summons is declared
  To meet the Judge with an unfearing heart.

Call it a vine, a rare and precious vine,
  Which, not a century since, was planted here,
Planted in faith and watched assidiously
  With anxious, alternating hope and fear;
Behold it now, a massive, fruitful thing,
  O'ershadowing e'en the borders of our State
At every compass point, and witnessing
  Each year a transformation still more great.

Blest evermore, be they—the pioneers
  Who bravely this great march of progress led;
Who struggled nobly through all doubts and fears,
  Till all uncertainity and doubt were dead.
May ceaseless benedictions on them fall;
  May heaven's high arches with their praise resound;
May all the deaf who live or are to live
  Cherish their names with reverence profound.

Blest be their names! and may their mantles fall
  Each generation upon spirits brave,

THE VENTURE.

Brave, eager to respond to Duty's call,
To toil, God's lowly ones to help, to save
From suffering in its many-sided forms
Of darkness, ignorance, sloth and shame and sin,
To guide them lovingly through earth's bleak storms
Safely the pearly gates of heaven within.

THE DEAF-MUTE ALUMNI REUNION.

From the city and the village,
From the hillside and the vale,
They have journeyed, they have gathered,
Stalwart men, and women frail,
Drawn together by a yearning
In their childhood's haunts to stand,
In a sacred Hall of learning
Lo! they meet—a goodly band.

Hands unclasped for years are shaken,
Hearts rejoice that long have wept,
Visions long forgot awaken
From some nook in which they slept;
Eyes will read in eyes the story
Of the hopes that soon decayed:
Friend to friend will show the records
Which the changeful years have made.

THE VENTURE.

Truthful memory is busy,
  Talking to each mind and heart,
Showing pictures, perfect pictures,
  Of the things that were apart
Of their being, when they gathered,
  Silent, trembling and afraid,
Here within these walls where learning
  Of them what they are has made.

Other forms than those around them
  Each one seems again to see;
Other faces smile upon them,
  Full of innocence and glee;
Teachers, school-mates, dead and living,
  They behold them all once more,
As they saw them, as they knew them
  In the happy days of yore.

Yet no one would change the present
  For those happy, careless hours,
All well know themselves the richer
  For emancipated powers.
Life and Time, then valued lightly,
  Now of precious worth are known,
And for promise, budding brightly,
  Lovely flowers and fruits are shown.

THE VENTURE.

Feeling this emancipation
  That a silent force has brought,
Conscious of the transformation
  That a little time has wrought,
Looking at the Past and Present,
  Joy and gratitude are blent,
And as incense to "Our Father,"
  Praise from every heart is sent.

Friendship will be stronger, purer,
  Faith in God and man more true,
Wisdom's final triumph surer,
  And this further good accrue—
Each with greater zeal will labor
  To make life a thing sublime,
And forever be the richer
  For this one reunion time.

There must come an hour of parting,
  But from it I turn away,
For before my mind is darting
  Visions of another day
When earth's silent ones shall gather
  In Our Father's House to dwell
Where their loosened tongues shall never
  Speak life's saddest word—"Farewell."

THE VENTURE. 37

THE PLEASURES OF REUNION.

They meet again, the man of years,
  The matron grave, the stalwart youth,
The maiden in whose face appears
  The proofs of innocence and truth.

And hands are clasped, or hard or soft,
  As different toils have set their seal,
And eyes and fingers question oft
  "What is your story, woe or weal?"

They meet, and while the moments whirl
  Laughter and smiles attest their joy,
The matron seems again a girl,
  The man a mischief-loving boy.

But that is all, no word is heard
  Which waiting echo might repeat,
To prove how much each heart is stirred
  Or that they hold reunion sweet.

For ears are deaf and tongues are dumb,
  Each has a life-long cross to bear;
The song of birds, the bees' grave hum
  Are pleasures which they may not share.

Yet sense sometimes grows more acute
  When to a double duty brought,

THE VENTURE.

Hands swiftly move, tho' lips be mute,
And signs may image every thought.

Therefore they meet again to-day,
Who met of old—a wordless band,
To tell how ignorance fled away
When Wisdom moved her gracious wand.

And praise the while the sovereign source
Of life and wisdom for the key
Which, while it moved with silent force,
From silence's chains has set them free.

They meet again who pledged to be
True friends in every time of need,
To own that Friendship is a sea
Whereon to launch and sail with heed.

They meet who spoke love's solemn vow,
Then broke it in a careless hour,
To read from eye and cheek and brow
Love is a thing of life-time power.

They meet again—but yet not all,
For here and there a vacant place
Gives answer when the roll we call
That death holds some in close embrace.

THE VENTURE. 39

Yet they and all who now are met
  May meet again, a perfect band,
And with no shadow of regret
  Before the Lord, "Our Father," stand.

There neither grieving nor appalled,
  That here they held reunion dear,
To answer when the roll is called
  The joyful chorus, "HERE, ALL HERE."

TO WHOM IS HONOR DUE?

Composed for the unveiling of a Memorial Portrait of Horatio
Nelson Hubbell, the first Superintendent of the Ohio Institution for
the Education of the Deaf and Dumb, and read at the Fifth Reunion
of its Alumni, held at Columbus, Ohio, September 1st to 3d, 1882.

Honor is not alone for those
  Who rule in haughty pomp and power,
For whom the people shout "long live,"
  And pay large tribute every hour.
No, no, else we might surely think
  Justice was growing basely partial,
And we, to check her foolish freak,
  Opposing influence must marshal.

Honor is not alone for those
  Who by some deed of strength or daring
Surprise the world and set the throng

THE VENTURE.

Wonderingly listening, talking, staring,
No, no, such may deserve some praise,
Embodied in a song or story,
But not to them in after days
Accrues the most enduring glory.

Unselfish labor for the weal
Of others—the oppressed, rejected,
The ignorant, isolated, who
So greatly, sadly, are afflicted,
In liberty, right and privilege,
Such as true souls deem worth securing,
This challenge, yes, this demands,
Honor most fervent, most enduring,

Better, ah! better far, to strive
With self-renouncing love to brighten
The lot of others; better far
Their sorrows, burdens, cares to lighten,
Than selfishly seek transient pleasure,
Or toil for wealth that any time
May vanish like the dew, the vapor,
The rainbow gay, the glittering rime.

Better, ah! better far, to live
Meek doers of some humble duty
That makes the world a happier place,

THE VENTURE.

41

Adds to its store of use and beauty,
  Than seek for fame in ways pronounced
By the cold-hearted, calculating,
  The safest, the most sure to prove
Quickly and largely compensating.

  Earth has no heroes more exalted
Than those who hold these doctrines true,
  Who prove their faith by boldly doing
Whatever Mercy bids them do,
  Be it to teach in voiceless manner,
Or act the foster-parent's part,
  Or do yet lowlier work, they merit
The honor of each grateful heart.

  Let no mean, sordid spirit whisper
"Waste not your means, they had their pay,"
  Gold is not full remuneration
For labor that affects alway,
  For blessings reaching outward upward,
Past earth, past time, so very far
  That God alone can know or measure
Exactly what their limits are.

  Say then, upon worth's hallowed altar
With grateful, willing, liberal hand,
  Memorials, graceful and substantial,

42 *THE VENTURE.*

Perpetuations that shall stand,
In silent eloquence attesting
We duly value, duly prize
All self-forgetting thought and labor
That tends to make us good and wise.

OPENING HYMN FOR THE SUNDAY SERVICES OF A DEAF-MUTE CONVENTION.

Deaf to all sound, we can not raise
Heavenward an oral hymn of praise,
Of doubly grateful praise that we
Once bound, benighted, now are free.

Free from afar with glad accord
To meet before our common Lord,
Free with our minds, our hearts, our hands
To yield the worship He demands.

Free in His Holy Word to read
The doctrine of one faith, one creed,
One church, its corner-stones to be
Truth, mercy, love and charity.

Free, any moment, anywhere,
With humble, importuning prayer
To turn to him, fully assured.
Christ has our audience secured.

THE VENTURE. 43

And we are sure that He, whose ear
  Even our secret thoughts can hear,
Will not disdain the voiceless praise
  Which we in rapturous concert raise.

Father Supreme, whose sovereign will
  Wisely decrees that we shall fill
A marked, peculiar people's place
  Witnessing to thy power, thy grace.

Now while we reverently adore
  Bless us each one, and more and more
Make us peculiar—all thine own,
  To live and toil for thee alone.

CLOSING HYMN FOR THE SAME SERVICES.

While sweet-toned organs proudly peal
  And millons of enchanted souls
In concert sing or meekly kneel
  Praising the being who controls
Omnipotently sea and land
  All nature, and celestial spheres;
Moves life and death by His command,
  And proves his power through all the years.

We, deaf to every oral sound,
  With voice untuned but heart aglow,

THE VENTURE.

With love and joy, intense, profound,
   Such as the grateful only know,
Have met to-day, a goodly band
   From near and far, that we may raise
With soul and mind and heart and hand
   Our voiceless songs of rapturous praise.

Father and Son and Spirit, deign
   To hear and to accept our song,
Baptize us all afresh and reign
   Supreme within us, making strong
Our faith, our trust, our love, our zeal,
   Oh, give us all the bread of grace,
The living water, so shall sin
   In us have less and less a place.

Long as we tarry here below
   Still be our refuge and our strength,
So shall we fear no ill, no foe,
   And more than conquerers, at length,
Shall in Thy glorious presence meet
   With ears unstopped and tongue unloosed
And praises manifold repeat,
   For powers here suppressed, refused.

THE VENTURE. **45**

ACROSTIC VERSES.

In memory of the Scotchman who is credited with the invention of the double hand alphabet, used exclusively by the Deaf and Dumb of England and Scotland, and to some extent in America.

Deeply on memory's tablet
 Engrave and gild his name,
Wreathe round it the best laurels
 True gratitude can frame.

Eulogize, praise, laud, honor,
 In all its sea-girt lands,
Where'er with palsied lip or ear
 A child despairing stands.

Lay it in history's pages
 With reverent, loving care,
And bid each generation
 Sacredly keep it there.

Gather all deaf and mute o nes,
 And, guided by his hands,
Repeat life's weighty lessons
 Till each one understands.

And show them how kind nature
 Compensates every ill
By giving counteracting power,
 Or substitutive skill.

THE VENTURE.

Raise them from degradation,
    Up, up the social plane,
Till all who see your labor,
    Concede it is not vain.

Nor cease, though slow the progress,
    Or very small the cheer;
Behold, admiring angels.
    Long as you toil, are near.

Oh, blessed, highly blessed,
    Are they among earth's sons,
Who bring emancipation
    To God's long-prisoned ones.

TO A DEAF-MUTE FOREIGNER.

Welcome, thrice welcome to our favored land,
    Illustrious stranger, through whose ears no sound,
However sweet or thrilling, loud or grand,
    Enters to break the silence most profound,
In which thy mind has dwelt through all the years
    It has been capable of hopes and fears.

Thrice welcome thou, whose lips could form no
        speech,
    Until the will, the brave, ambitious will,
Determined nature it would ever reach.

THE VENTURE.

Low at the foot of Difficulty's Hill,
Vowed, "nothing daunted by its height, I'll press
Up to the pinnacle of proud success."

Welcome, thrice welcome, as a brilliant proof
That earnest effort is not thrown away,
And if we rightly prize life's curious woof
And weave its web with care from day to day,
Our rich reward will some day surely be
A fabric from defects wondrously free.

Welcome, as teacher of the sacred truth
That diligence in business often brings
Men, even in their days of early youth,
Into the presence of earth's mightiest kings,
Engraves in golden characters their name,
And crowns them with the laurel wreath of fame.

Welcome, great heart, that never scorns to own
A brother, though his garb be poor or plain,
That, though it never hears an anguished moan,
Deems it a joy to lessen care and pain,
And prove, when men are bordering on despair,
That God doth kindly hear and answer prayer.

Welcome, and if it please thee, tarry long,
For we have need of spirits such as thine,
To aid us in our struggles against wrong,

48 *THE VENTURE.*

And teach us never idly to repine,
E'en though we bear a very heavy cross,
  And sound low depths of sorrow and of loss.

Welcome, and may the God who guided thee
  Across the pathless ocean to our shore,
Thy Friend, thy Guide, and loving Guardian be,
  Giving thee back, redoubled o'er and o'er,
Thy bounty, and when life's full span is run,
  May angel hosts sing thee His pleased "Well
    done."

TO A HEBREW DEAF-MUTE.

Waiting, brother, waiting,
  For Messiah, King,
Who to Israel's children
  Freedom, joy, will bring,
He has come, though lowly,
  And in every zone
Holiest of the holy,
  Waits to set his throne.

Hoping, brother, hoping
  For the promised light
That will end forever
  The long, dismal night,

THE VENTURE. 49

Law and prophets fasten
  Round the dense and drear,
With but expectation
  Heart and mind to cheer.

Give thy hoping over,
  It is useless now,
And in reverent homage
  To Immanuel bow,
For the light is beaming
  O'er all longing ones,
Brighter than the gleaming
  Of a million suns.

Longing, brother, longing,
  For a fountain sweet,
For pure, living waters
  And a rest complete,
Lo! a fount is flowing,
  Copious and free,
Rest and peace are offered
  Without price to thee.

Seeking, brother, seeking
  For the royal way
To the heavenly Canaan,
  To the perfect day. ·

THE VENTURE.

Seek, Oh, seek no longer,
  For the way is found,
Narrow, straight, but wholly
  Consecrated ground.

Hoping, waiting, longing,
  Seeking, all, give o'er,
Lo! Messiah opens
  Wide the Gospel door.
Leave the types and shadows
  For the substance real,
For the Christ is mighty
  To redeem and heal.

Hasten, brother, hasten,
  Time is flying fast,
Mercy's calls are echoing
  In each beeeze and blast,
Hasten now to Jesus,
  Jesus crucified,
And thy soul's deep longing
  Shall be satisfied.

THE VENTURE. 51

HYMNS

For the unveiling of a Memorial Tablet, erected by
Deaf-Mutes to a former teacher.

FIRST.

The crowd may laud as heroes
  Those who with weapons gory,
From long-contested battle-fields
  March, claiming meeds of glory;
May shout for them "Hurrah! hurrah!"
  May bow with admiration,
And to official titles add
  Most flattering commendation;
May wail when they are summoned
  To join the myriad dead,
And mark with costly marble
  Their deep sepulchral bed.

But while such may be worthy
  All their adherents claim,
'Tis not for them the wise of earth
  Decree most lasting fame;
'Tis not to them the troubled look
  When wrongs demand redress;
Not them, when Right has triumphed
  We with most unction bless;
'Tis not for them when they must die

THE VENTURE.

The grateful sorely grieve;
Nor for them admiring angels
Their finest chaplets weave.

But they who at the promptings
 Of conscience, bravely go
To the cheerless haunts of ignorance,
 Of folly, sin and woe;
Go with the lamp of knowledge
 For those who blindly grope,
With promises of mercy
 For those who have no hope,
With the living Bread and Water
 For the hungry and the faint,
With the balm of consolation
 For all who have a plaint.

Such are earth's greatest heroes,
 Her bravest, noblest men,
Worthy the adulation
 Of every tongue and pen,
Worthy the painter's highest skill,
 The sculptor's truest art;
Worthy the loving memory
 Of every grateful heart.
Whether their mode be pantomime,

THE VENTURE.

Or strangely foreign speech,
Or native language, Heaven's smile
Attends each word they teach.

SECOND.

Do we not err to call them dead
Who after years of zealous toil
To lessen human woe and spread
Light, sound and knowledge, and to foil
Evil in its deep-plotted schemes,
Obey the All-Beholding One,
And calmly as the fading beams
Of sunlight, when the day is done,
Slip from their tenements of clay
And pass from mortal sight away.

Surely we err, for spirit, like
Its great originator, is
Immortal. Vile decay may strike
The flesh and proudly claim it his,
But spirit, ransomed spirit, knows
No death, once set at liberty,
It seeks its source, expands and grows
In glorious power and symmetry,
Yet to our yearning questioning
Returns in loving ministring.

THE VENTURE.

Return in dreary, troubled hours,
  Gently as sunbeams meet the dew,
To fill our hands with hope's sweet flowers,
  And picture to our spirits' view
Reminders of the love divine
  That follows us with tireless care
To smooth, to straighten and define,
  To banish darkness and despair;
That robs of terror e'en the grave,
And will with full salvation save.

But though when leaving earth they pause
  Kindly to say, "The path is light,
For weeping there will be no cause,
  God rules, and His decrees are right,"
Gratitude suffers us to grieve
  Over the loss we feel immense,
And as a proof the sighs we heave
  Spring from no shallow, base pretense,
Bids us their sculptured name and face
  Give in God's house an honored place.

And bids us when we pass within
  Its sacred portals, call to mind
The truths by which they strove to win
  Our souls from evil, and to bind
Us all to good, Oh, doubly blest

THE VENTURE.

Are they who point earth's wandering ones
To the true source of peace and rest,
  God owns them as his bravest sons,
And blest by Him, each truth they taught
  Shall live in noble deed or thought.

HYMN

For the dedication of a chapel for Deaf Mutes.

Hungering for the bread of God,
  Fresh from His benignant hand,
For the manna of His love,
  Found in every age and land;
Thirsting for the water sweet
  Flowing from the fount of life,
Potent to refresh and nerve
  Souls for noble toil and strife.

Seeking for that better way
  That leads on to Heaven's rest,
Looking for the light that grows
  Brighter for Time's every test,
Knowing that whate'er our state
  For us all one Saviour died,
For us all he rose again
  Ever to be glorified.

56   *THE VENTURE.*

We have gathered here to-day,
    A devout, though voiceless, band,
Humbly at God's feet to lay
    The best gifts at our command;
Gathered here to dedicate
    One more altar, one more shrine,
Unto Him whom we adore
    As all mighty, all divine.

Deign, Thou Sovereign, One in Three,
    Deign our offering to accept;
Henceforth may it ever be
    Sacred to Thy service kept,
May we here rich treasures find,
    Here in grace and wisdom grow,
And in spirit, heart and mind
    Onward to perfection go.

TO A DEAF-MUTE LADY.

We met but once, just for a little while,
And ever since that hour, deep in my heart
Your name has lain inscribed indeliably,
And in the picture gallery of my mind
Your image has retained a worthy place,
And I will gaze upon it in the days
That yet may add unto my span of life,

THE VENTURE.

My knowledge and the number of my friends.
The modest grace, the cordial sympathy
Revealed both by your countenance and words,
Roused in my heart a tender, latent chord
That then vibrated, and is vibrating
Even yet, most pleasantly.
Our meetings and our partings may be termed
A matter of small consequence, but life, you know,
Is made of little things, and spirits grow
By slow degrees, yet ever quickly note
Affinity, wherever it exists,
In any one they casually may meet,
And so it was with me that long ago
I saw in you a spirit that aspired
Above, beyond herself, and so my heart
Thrilled with a sense of true affinity,
And owns to-day that it is richer for
Those moments spent with you.

"I PRAYED FOR YOU."

"Last night I prayed for you," a mute child said,
  With finger-letters, then she went her way,
And I, to whom she spoke, I bowed my head
  And wept for joy that she for me should pray,
For I was doubting, and my heart was sore,

THE VENTURE.

Life seemed a struggle, hardly worth its cost,
My stars of hope seemed set to rise no more,
And much that others prized to me was lost.

"Last night I prayed for you," the simple words
Seemed like a message from the spirit shore,
Or like the sweetest songs of wild wood birds,
And thrilled me to my being's very core
Till life, that seemed ere while so hard and cold
Grew warm and precious, and my heart grew
strong,
Meekly to drink all that my cup might hold,
And toil with patience, though my task were long.

"Last night I prayed for you!" If those whose
tongues
Can speak no sinful words, for us will pray,
What need we fear our heart-strings may be wrung
By bitter grief or pain from day to day,
Yet strength and help shall never, never fail,
For God doth ever love the young and pure,
And they have power with him and shall prevail
So long as his own word remaineth sure.

Oh, mighty is the worth, the power of prayer
To heal the heart when grief has made it bleed,
To ease the mind when bowed by heavy care,

THE VENTURE. 59

Or bring us help in every time of need,
To banish doubt and make the spirit strong,
  Aye, make it patient, trustful, calm and brave,
To tune the dirge to sweet, exultant song,
  And strew with flowers the death-bed and the
    grave.

Pray then, all ye who know there is a God
  Ruling and reigning throughout earth and Heaven;
Pray when you groan beneath the chastening rod;
  Pray, too, when rest and joy to you are given;
Pray for your friends, whatever be their state,
  They need God's grace and guidance every hour.
That they all good may love, all evil hate,
  And meet defiantly the tempter's power.

THE MARCH OF PROGRESS.

The red man and the deer have fled,
  The wolf's wild howl is heard no more,
The "fort" has to a city spread,
  The stream is spanned from shore to shore,
The steam-horse wends its rapid way
  O'er hill and valley, mead and plain,
And for the wilderness to-day
  We see vast fields, where precious grain

THE VENTURE.

Yearly repays all seed-time toil
   And harvest-hours of thoughtful care.

Churches, too, lift their steeples high
   And throw their portals open wide,
While for the frightful battle-cry
   Of savage warriors, side by side
Aliens walk, singing as they go
   Of mutual interest, mutual hope,
Pledging support in weal or woe,
   Vowing they will together cope
Till every danger shall have passed
   And they have conquered every foe.

And school-bells ring their daily call
   For youth to walk in wisdom's ways,
And prove through useful years that all
   Persistent mental culture pays;
That zeal with aspiration pure
   Commands respect and will at last
Success attain, reward secure,
   Exert an influence, small or vast,
Even though the waiting may be long,
   A glorious reaping time is sure.

And science gathers up vast stores
   Of curious things from mounts and mines,

THE VENTURE. 61

From hills and glades and river shores
  From shrubs and bushes, plants and vines,
Classifies them and spreads them out,
  And bids the hurrying throng to pause
And note each strange phenomenon,
  Each consequence of law and cause,
Note and acknowledge power divine
  Rules over all the universe.

And art, uniquest, truest proof
  Of talent, rears her temples high,
Trying alike by web and woof,
  By form and hue to please the eye,
To please the fancy in its flights,
  By restless reachings after grace,
Symmetry, beauty, everything
  Which bears the least æsthetic trace,
Fills, crams her deftly-shapen halls
  Till every inch of space is full.

And mind, when it would speak to mind,
  Defiant laughs at time and space,
And sends its words, cruel or kind
  Straight on to their intended place,
Sends them with swiftest lightning speed
  Through mid-air or the ocean's heart,
And every hour, by will decreed,

THE VENTURE.

Thought answers thought, tho' miles apart,
As spirits telegraph afar
　　Their joy or grief, their hope or fear.

Truth, too, and Reason rear aloft
　　Their gracious beacons, and declare
That though assailed and trammeled oft,
　　Heaven has for them a special care,
Envy and hatred, spite and pride,
　　Falsehood and malice, all the throng
Of evils which make up the tide
　　We call injustice, error, wrong,
All, all must yield, must surely yield,
　　Leaving them in triumphant sway.

And Wisdom, true religion's twin
　　With schools alone not satisfied,
With the progressive train falls in,
　　Sends out her agents far and wide,
To gather up with careful hands
　　Thoughts that ennoble and refine,
Instruct and please, aye, from all lands
　　To gather gems from Truth's rich mine,
And placing what they bring in ranks,
　　In groups, in piles, invites the crowd,

THE VENTURE. 63

Invites the restless, eager crowd
  To the rare feasts of precious lore,
Calls them in tones now low, now loud,
  To come, nor roam nor hunger more,
Howe'er their taste or fancy turn
  To stars or stones, to plane or line,
To substances that freeze or burn,
  To natures human or divine,
She spreads her stores with generous hand
  Bidding all use till satisfied.

Invites, too, beings once supposed
  Beyond the reach of hope or prayer,
The blind, whose eyes are ever closed,
  The deaf and dumb, denied a share
In speech and sound, and others who
  With imbeciles were wont to mope,
She calls to learn with pleasure true
  That they no longer need to grope
In mental darkness, but can keep
  Fair pace in the progressive march.

Clay-beds and sand-banks next we find
  Transformed to many useful things
To suit the rich or the refined,
  The heirs of peasants or of kings,

THE VENTURE.

Iron-. ⸳ ⸳. alabaster-white,
  Or delicate as morning dew,
Of crystal clearness, noonday light,
  Or showing every tint and hue
Of every kind and every mould
  Which errant fancy can devise.

Ores, too, and metals, deftly wrought
  Accomplish in a single hour
Work which past generations thought
  Nothing could do but human power.
Propelled by steam's superior force
  Shuttles and needles swiftly fly,
Planes move in keen, unwavering course,
  Saws, hammers, chisels all defy
All human strength or speed and prove
  The worth of mind, the power of thought.

The very soil on which we live
  Joins the immense, progressive train
At labor's call, and hastes to give
  Each season, in rich stores of grain,
Of fruit or flowers, the tribute due
  To talent, energy and skill,
The proof that blessings must accrue
  When we by honest toil so will,

THE VENTURE.

When God approving smiles and bids
    The rain to fall, the sun ... b... e.
The very light by which we move
    When Night her sable mantle throws
Over the world, unites to prove
    The power of thought, and to disclose
The fact that very many things
    Once counted powerless, useless, hold
Vast latent forces, which, evolved,
    Cause revolutions manifold,
And place round the discoverer's name
    Unfading laurel wreaths of fame.

The very graves o'er which we weep
    For precious loved ones passed away,
Pace in this march of progress keep
    And swell the wonderful array
Of beauteous and substantial things
    Which are proof-patent every hour
That every age in passing brings
    Our age, our nation, added power
From failures to achieve success,
    And to the world grand records leave.

THE BLIND DEAF-MUTE.

Deaf, dumb and blind! It seems so hard, so hard,
    No sound, no sound, silence on every side;

THE VENTURE.

Silence, as perfect, utter and profound
    As reigned when chaos yawned, deep, dark and wide.

Deaf, dumb and blind!   It seems so hard, so hard,
    Dumb, though the mind be all ablaze with thought;
Dumb, though the spirit's tenderest depths and heights
    Are into ecstacy or frenzy wrought.

Deaf, dumb and blind! It seems so strange, so strange,
    No light, no light, forever in the dark,
Darkness most dense, wide as the world is wide,
    With no relieving glimmer, ray or spark.

Deaf dumb and blind!   Alone, wholly alone,
    Shut up in the small prison of herself,
Resembling much a book firm closed and clasped
    And tossed as useless upon Mystery's shelf.

And yet, perchance, she dwells not quite alone,
    Angels may be her visitants and friends,
Or at the dear Lord's pitying commands
    Often the Comforter to her descends.

And it may be her spirit senses all
    Keener than ours, pierce the celestial spheres.
And while we pitying say, "Deaf, dumb and blind!"
    Rare sights delight her eyes, rare sounds her ears.

THE VENTURE. 67

A STRANGE HALF-CENTURY.

Suggested by the remark of Laura D. Bridgman, in a letter written September 15, 1879, while she was visiting her mother at the old homestead in Hanover, N. H.:
"My birthday is on the 21st of December—fifty years old!"

Almost fifty years of *darkness*,
   Darkness deep as ever fell
O'er the world at day's declining,
   With its wierd and waking spell,
Darkness so intense no glimmer
   Were all Nature's lights combined
With all lights of man's inventing
   E'er could reach the imprisoned mind.
     Yet she wails no question "why?"
     Satsified that by and bye
     Time with emphasis will tell:
     "Though so trying, it was well."

Almost fifty years of *silence*,
   Silence utter and profound,
As if Nature had grown powerless
   To produce a single sound,·
As if all the air was muffled
   Or had lost resounding force,
Lost all power to carry echoes
   Or reveal their primal source.

THE VENTURE.

Yet she wails no question, "why?"
Satisfied that by and bye
Time with emphasis will tell:
"Though so lonely, it was well."

Almost fifty years unable
  Rightly to articulate
Exclamations, questions, answers,
  Which would show the spirit's state,
Would reveal its joy or sorrow,
  Show its cause for hope and fear,
Tell why mirth gives place to sadness,
  Or why falls the pearly tear.
    Yet she wails no question, "why?"
    Satisfied that by and bye
    Time with emphasis will tell:
    "Though so grevious, it was well."

Almost fifty years of toiling,
  Toiling patiently to gain
Word by word, the common knowledge
  Others rapidly attain;
Word by word, the truth that reason
  Holds and will forever hold
Far more precious than earth's treasures
  Multiplied to countless fold.
    Yet she wails no question, "why?"

THE VENTURE. 69

Satisfied that by and bye
Time with emphásis will tell:
"Though so tedious, it was well."

Almost fifty years of groping,
Groping cautiously about,
Pausing oftentimes in terror,
Oftener still in dread or doubt,
Wondering if the sun is shining,
Or if clouds the sky obscure,
If the evening lamp is lighted,
Or the food and drink are pure.
Yet she wails no question, "why?"
Satisfied that by and bye
Time with emphasis will tell:
"Though so wearying, it was well."

Almost fifty years of striving
To win victory from defeat,
Make a prosy fate a poem
Millions proudly shall repeat,
Make for scholars and for skeptics
Theories and questions strange,
Arguments and views perplexing
When from God they dare to range.
Yet she wails no question, "why?"
Satisfied that by and bye

THE VENTURE.

Time with emphasis will tell:
"Though so mysterious, it was well."

Almost fifty years attesting
  We are not the work of chance,
But the heirs of One who ever
  Bids us rise, achieve, advance,
Bids us show by wise improval
  Of our talents, small or great,
We may not one jot nor tittle
  Of our Maker's praise abate.
    Yet she wails no question, "why?"
    Satisfied that by and bye
    Time with emphasis will tell:
    "Though so onerous, it was well."

Almost fifty years declaring
  Mind is mighty and will rise,
From the wreck of sense and venture
  Boldly after crown and prize,
Venture, strive, aspire and struggle
  Conquer, persevere and stand
On the lofty heights of triumph,
  Known and praised in many a land.
    Yet she wails no question, "why?"
    Satisfied that by and bye

THE VENTURE. 71

Time with emphasis will tell:
"God decreed all, it was well."

Almost fifty years of hoping
For the morning that shall end
The protracted night of trials
Which so clearly, strangely, blend
End the slow and cautious groping
End the isolation sore,
End the wondering and the longing
End them all forevermore.
Yet she wails no question, "why?"
Satisfied that by and bye
Time with emphasis will tell:
"*All that God decrees is well.*"

A CHALLENGE.

Ho! Ye that pass by on the smooth ways of Time,
Complacently saying, "'Tis nothing to me—
Nothing at least having semblance of crime,
If while I am journeying, favored and free,
Prisoners most abject moan, wearily moan
And long for liberty, liberty sweet,
Long till their feelings find vent in a gloom
So deep that its anguish were hard to repeat."

THE VENTURE.

Speak not so proudly, the souls that you meet
    Burdened by sorrow or trouble or care,
Defiled by the dust or the mire of the street,
    Or driven by want to the brink of despair,
Are brothers and sisters, whose miserable state
    Always is something, something to you,
And sometime, alas! should that sometime be late,
    You will find you to each have a duty to do.

The deaf and the dumb, standing sadly apart,
    Never once cheered by an audible sound,
Whatever the longing of mind or of heart,
    Doomed to live on in their silence profound;
The blind groping cautiously, or in affright
    Shunning one danger, another to meet,
Or moodily waiting the end of their night,
    So tedious, so long, so intensely complete.

The lunatic's raving is mental unrest,
    More torturing far than physical pain;
The gibbering idiot, who at the best
    Wakes and eats but to sink to its slumbers again;
The fallen, repentant, who timidly shrink
    From the withering scorn and self-satisfied pride
Of the throng, and the wrecked, who, too hopeful to
    sink,
    Too despairing to sail, drift along with the tide.

THE VENTURE. 73

The widow, who wearily toils to protect
　Her innocent children from hunger and cold;
The sick and the maimed, often doomed to neglect,
　The lone, the deserted, the feeble, the old,
The strangers, the exiled from country and home,
　Who uncared for, passed by and neglected alway,
Are forced by misfortune to restlessly roam
　Till nature's last debt they are summoned to pay.

All these have a claim on your thoughts and your
　　care,
　All these challenge daily your pity and aid,
And as you deny or accord them a share,
　Are as witnesses for or against you arrayed.
Then say not again, "It is nothing to me,"
　Lest the selfish assertion be echoed in Heaven,
And Justice sends back the indignant decree:
　"Your sin is too great to be quickly forgiven."

TEMPERANCE POEMS.

THE VENTURE. 75

THE WHISKY-JUG'S REVELATION.

Here is plenty of poverty, shame and disgrace,
 An imbecile mind and a red, bloated face,
A cold, stony heart and a trembling hand,
 A strong man so feeble he scarcely can stand.
Friend, look at these pictures awhile e're you pass,
 They cost little money—just ten cents a glass.

Here are dirt and disorder, starvation and cold,
 And misery greater than words ever told;
Here are anger and hatred, contention and strife,
 A hell for a home and existence for life.
Friends, think of these evils awhile e're you pass,
 And say if you'll buy them at ten cents a glass.

Here are ruin, damnation, remorse and despair,
 Aye, wretchedness greater than words can declare,
Long ages of pain for short moments of mirth,
 Souls bitterly cursing the hour of their birth.
O! friend, dare you suffer such warnings to pass,
 And swallow destruction at ten cents a glass?

"THE PLEASANT GLASS."

Composed after reading the remark of a deaf-mute:
"We went into a saloon to take a pleasant glass."

O, look not on the "pleasant glass,"
 Though it most brightly gleams,

THE VENTURE.

For with a curse, a woe untold,
    Its every golbule teems.

O, touch it not, the "pleasant glass,"
    Though good it be to view,
For it with sharp and cruel thorns
    Your path of life can strew.

O, drink it not, the "pleasant glass,"
    Though warm and sweet it taste,
For it has power to work more ill
    Than pencil ever traced.

O, dash it down, the "pleasant glass,"
    As poison, ruin, death,
Turn quickly from it as you would
    Turn from the spoiler's breath.

Yes, dash it down, until it lies
    In fragments at your feet,
For only thus will you escape
    From ruin be complete.

And call it not the "pleasant glass,"
    For ruined millions know
That *poisoned*, CURSED, are fitter words
    Its subtle power to show.

THE VENTURE.

A PLEA.

After reading of a drunkard who was highly connected and held
honorable position in the army, the account ending with the remark,
"He is a ruined man."

Call him not ruined while life's tide is flowing
    Warm through his veins,
And reason, by sure signs, is daily showing
    It still retains
Its throne within the mind once strong and noble,
    Once brave and true,
To will and plan, direct, command and venture,
    Decide and do.

Call him not wholly ruined, noble brothers,
    You, who are strong,
Temptations to resist, and bravely battle
    With vice and wrong,
Hasten to him and kindly tell him, others
    Who fall, arise,
Regain all they had lost and add unto it
    Much which men prize.

Call him not ruined, though so lowly fallen,
    Remember that
While there is life, hope firmly may be cherished
    Still to combat,
Resist and re-resist the tempter's sieges,

78 *THE VENTURE.*

Man has grown strong,
And joins, from degradation resurected,
Earth's noble throng.

Call him not ruined, tell him of his darlings,
His parents dear,
His brothers, sisters, friends and soldier comrades,
Then when a tear
Drops from his eye, speak tenderly, speak softly,
Of wife and child,
Who love him still, and wait to kiss him welcome,
Though so defiled.

Call him not ruined, tho' so nearly perished,
Remember that
While life remains hope rightly may be cherished,
And we combat
With men or demons who with selfish fury
Struggle and strive
Away from God and all things pure and holy,
To drag or drive.

HELP THE DRUNKARD TO REFORM.

Scorn not the drunkard if he falls,
But reach him out a helping hand,
Set him upon his feet again,

THE VENTURE. 79

And bid him try again to stand.
  Tell him that as the little child
First learns to walk, so he must learn
  Each time he falls to rise again,
And from temptation bravely turn.

  Tell him that effort is the price
Of all success, and he must try
  Over and over, till he grows
Able to pass temptation by,
  Able to say the firm word, " No,"
And stick to it, whoever sneers,
  Able to be a brave, true man,
In spite of ridicule or jeers.

  Tell him that millions daily pray
For him and every tempted one,
  That Heaven waits to give him grace
Temptation to resist and shun,
  Aye, tell him this, and tell him more,
But never pass him by with scorn,
  Lest he, despairing, fall again,
Cursing the hour that he was born.

  Scorn not the drunkard, tho' he fall,
He is thy brother, just the same,
  And holds upon thy love and aid

THE VENTURE.

A double, yes, a treble claim.
  While life continues, there is hope
That reason will assert its sway,
  Will with temptation bravely cope,
And gloriously your toil repay.

FOR GOD AND HUMANITY.

"To arms!" Behold, a cruel foe
Is marching boldly through our land,
  Laying our noble brothers low
And scattering woe on every hand.

  "To arms! to arms!" Lo, widows pale
With grief and want, repeat the cry;
  While hosts of children sadly wail:
"Haste, haste, to arms! We starve, we die!"

  "To arms! to arms!" By all the throng
That dwells in Heaven, forever blest,
  The solemn charge is sent along:
"To arms! nor pause in selfish rest."

  "To arms! to arms!" From countless souls
Writhing in anguish and despair
  The charge in constant echo rolls
Like thunder peals through all the air.

THE VENTURE. 81

"To arms!" the arms of earnest work
For prohibition, haste away,
　For while you argue, pause and shirk,
Millions are ruined—lost for aye.

"To arms! to arms!" by God's own voice
The charge in firm command is given.
　Haste, help the whole world to rejoice,
Haste, help to swell the hosts of Heaven.

LOCAL POEMS.

"THE BELL IS TOLLING."

Toll the bell, slow and clear,
   Toll it so that all may hear,
Hear and know another soul
   Has at last attained a goal,
Has life's mighty problem solved,
   All its partnerships dissolved,
And is resting calmly now,
   While in tears its loved ones bow,
      Toll the bell.

Toll the bell, four, five and ten,
   See the miniature twin-men,
Sleeping, playing, side by side,
   Dreaming earth is wondrous wide;
Counting o'er their books and toys,
   Making mother cares and joys,
Thinking life is sweet and gay,
   Age and death are far away,
      Toll the bell.

Twenty, thirty, next we hear,
   Hands are strong and heads are clear,
Brothers still in peace abide,
   Dwelling, toiling, side by side,
Giving honest weight to all,

THE VENTURE.

Counting true for large and small,
Planning, venturing, with a will,
  Proving each the other's skill,
    Toll the bell.

Forty, fifty, how the years
  Multiply their hopes and fears,
Bring us wealth and holy joy,
  Bring us grief and sore annoy,
Bring us age and silvered hair,
  Stamp our brows with lines of care,
Come and vanish, day by day,
  Bearing us with them away,
    Toll the bell.

Fifty-six! one more were seven,
  Think we now of death and Heaven,
For the Captain's work is done,
  All his span of life is run,
Vain is the physician's art,
  Death has touched his brain and heart,
From his lips has forced the cry:
  "All is over, *I must die!*"
    Toll the bell.

Now a brother walks alone,
  Now a widow makes sad moan,

THE VENTURE. 85

Now we hear a mother sigh:
"Ever do the dearest die;"
Now for children's merry glee,
  Sobs we hear and tears we see,
Yet the promise sweet is given:
"There is love and rest in Heaven,"
Richer boon we can not crave,,
    Toll the bell and mark the grave.

BABY BERTHA.

Once and only once I saw her,
  And then I thought her much
Like a rare bud destined to blast
  At the first chilling touch.

Once and only once I held her,
  And then I seemed to hold
An angel waiting for its wings,
  Its crown and harp of gold.

And so it proved, the tender bud
  Grew tenderer every day,
Till white and cold as falling snow,
  Void of all power it lay.

THE VENTURE.

But the pure soul that gave it life,
 With wings full grown and strong,
Passed upward from all mortal sight
 To swell the angel throng.

To share with them the genial home
 Where pain and grief and tears
Can never hurt or fright as here,
 Through all the countless years.

Ye who that bud, that angel, prized,
 Who hoped that it might grow
To full perfection in your home,
 Your garden here below,

Weep, if you will, to ease your hearts,
 But while you weep, rejoice
That God for your fair darling's made
 A wiser, better choice.

PARENTAL LAMENT ON THE DEATH OF TWIN BOYS.

We looked for one, but two were sent
 To tax our thought and care,
To claim within our love and home
 An equal place and share,

THE VENTURE. 87

And though surprised, we did not turn
  Either in scorn away,
But welcomed both and watched with joy
  Their growth from day to day.

We gave them each a pretty name,
  And talked of many a plan
That would their interests advance
  As child and youth and man,
And we were sure, were very sure,
  That in the world's vast round
Two dearer little twins than ours
  Were nowhere to be found.

Thus the bright, happy weeks went by,
  Till half a year was told,
When suddenly our little boys
  Grew ill and pale and cold,
And from our doting sight were borne
  In quiet, solemn state,
Leaving us with our blighted hopes,
  Our desolation great.

To go all day with empty arms
  Seems very strange indeed,
And though we try to be resigned,
  Our hearts will ache and bleed.

THE VENTURE.

And when night's heavy shadows fall
  And we retire to rest,
We miss the baby heads we used
  To pillow on our breast.

OUR FRIEND.

"To know her was to love her," she was fair
As the fair flowers she loved so well to tend,
And from her life there floated a perfume
Sweet as the odor of the choicest rose,
Or lilies of the valley that e'er shed
Their choice perfume upon the ambient air.

To know her was to know that she was true,
As ever is the needle to the pole,
Or north star to the night, or song of bird
To the returning Spring, or brooding dove
Is to its mate, yea, in a high degree
True as "Our Father" bids us to be true.

To know her was to wish to emulate;
Her life was beautiful by deeds of love;
Kind words where'er her pathway chanced to lay,
Were echoed forth like sweet, harmonious notes,
And waked glad melodies in many hearts
That had grown sick with discord, pain and strife.

THE VENTURE. 89

To know her was to grieve that one so good
Should leave the world so soon, for it has need
Of such pure souls to make it something like
The Eden that it was e'er sin indulged
Had wrought the transformation we behold
Around us, and would alter if we could.

IN REMEMBRANCE.

Call her a flower, for she was fair;
  Call her a star, for she was bright;
Call her a jewel, rich and rare;
  Call her an angel and a light.

And we are sure you will not wrong
  Those flowers which in their forms and hue
Outrival all the floral throng,
  And lavishly their perfume strew.

Nor will you wrong those brilliant things
  Which dot the sky whenever night
Kindly outspreads her sable wings
  To give us rest from toil and light.

Nor will you wrong one precious gem
  Which brightly gleams or softly glows,

THE VENTURE.

In casket or in diadem,
   As light upon it ebbs or flows.

Nor will you wrong those seraphs bright
   Who highest in the heavenly throngs,
Guide them to scenes of new delight
   And lead them in their grandest songs.

We loved our flower, admired our star,
   And duly prized our jewel rare,
We thought through many a trying hour
   Our angel wondrous wise and fair.

And hoped, how fondly none can know
   But those whom hope no longer cheers,
Our flower would bloom, our star would glow,
   Our jewel shine for years and years.

But in a dark, a dismal hour,
   The angel, Death, with jealous eye,
Looked on our flower, our beauteous flower,
   And sternly bade her droop and die.

Looked on our star, our jewel bright,
   And took her radiance all away,
And left her lying still and white,
   Cold as a stone, or lump of clay.

THE VENTURE. 91

Looked on our Light, our angel one,
  And pointing her to happier spheres,
Told her she was forever done
  With toil and sorrow, pain and tears.

Told her to hasten, nor to wait
  Our farewell kiss, our fond good-bye,
For sometime it would be our fate
  Like her to droop and fade and die.

Oh, sad, Oh, solemn as the night
  When first we knew that she was dead!
We hold that Sabbath day so bright
  When first we made her earthly bed.

Yet, tell us not, Oh, tell us not
  Within that cold and silent tomb,
Which yet we hold a sacred spot,
  Despite its lonely, solemn gloom,

All, all that made our flower so sweet,
  Our star, our jewel, so divine,
Our light our angel, so complete,
  Moulders, no more to bloom or shine.

For hope and faith, that blessed twain,
  Commissioned sorrowing hearts to cheer,

THE VENTURE.

Turn from the grave as in disdain,
  And say, "Rejoice, all is not here.

" *All is not here*, the immortal soul
  Which made your darling's grace and worth
Lives, and shall live while ages roll
  And you are done with time and earth."

THE EARLY DEAD.

Joy cometh and we fold it
  Close to our throbbing heart,
And pray that we may never
  With it be forced to part.

Or form we deem angelic
  Knocks softly at the door,
We open, bid it enter,
  And tarry evermore.

Hope strengthens love's desires,
  And to our angel guest
We sing our sweetest measures
  Of lullaby and rest.

Nor cease our loving labors,
  Though it, earth-weary, try

THE VENTURE. 93

With restless fever-flutterings,
From us away to fly.

Nor scarce believe our senses
When to our eager cries
For it, nothing but echo
Or vacancy replies.

Yet, while we miss the body,
So early doomed to die,
We know the soul is happy
In spheres beyond the sky.

SUGGESTIONS.

If we could always keep the forms we prize,
Earth, now so desolated, soon would be
Heaven's counterpart, and we, with tearless eyes
Would speak of Heaven and of Eternity.

No thoughts of sweet reunion by and bye,
Would rouse within us longings to be pure,
Nor nerve us with courageous zeal to try
Time's tests and trials bravely to endure.

And where we now have cherished images
Of lovely children and well-guarded graves,

94

THE VENTURE.

We would have grown folks, always growing old,
And, like ourselves, to toil and trouble slaves.

So it is well that Death doth jealously
Look on our darlings, and bid some depart
To people Heaven; constrain us to be wise,
Fear God and serve Him with a perfect heart.

PARENTS' TREASURES.

A picture fair and true
Of a child-face we thought more sweet and dear
Than any other that we ever knew
Within the whole world's compass, far or near.

A lock of silken hair,
Some toys and little garments laid away,
And guarded with a mother's tender care,
As treasures much too precious for decay.

A grave wherein is laid
A childish form that we were wont to fold
Close to our hearts, thinking we would not trade
Nor barter it for tons of glittering gold.

Just there where we had hoped
For long possession and devoted care,

THE VENTURE.

For noble growth, for honor, joy and pride,
And a brave voice to echo praise and prayer.

Just there, yet something more,
Sweet thoughts that cheer and comfort all our
    grief,
Our child awaits us on the spirit shore,
The hours fly fast, and life, at most, is brief.

THE DEAD MOTHER.

Close the dear eyes,
So brilliantly bright,
    With love's pure, thrilling,
Heaven-fed light.

Smooth the soft hair
As she used to each day,
    Reserving a tress
With your treasures to lay.

Fold the white hands,
Grown so thin and so weak,
    With daily endeavors
Our profit to seek.

THE VENTURE.

Kiss the cold lips,
Though they answer no more,
Breathe a glad prayer
That their quivering is o'er.

Think of her virtues,
Her amiable ways,
Emulate till
You deserve equal praise.

Cherish her memory
Wherever you stray,
And speak of her gratefully,
Fondly, alway.

TO MOTHERS.

Oh, mothers! when your little ones
With all their infant charms,
Are taken by the Angel, Death,
From out your loving arms,
If in my eyes you see no tears,
Nor find a single trace
Of grief because they went away,
Imaged upon my face,

THE VENTURE.

Accuse me not of heartlessness,
Nor call me proud and cold,
Careless when others' hearts are bowed
With bitterness untold,
For while I know—and know full well
Your hearts are sad and sore,
With longings for the little forms
Who claim your care no more,

I know as well, this world is full
Of sorrow, pain and woe,
And that the tempter spreads his snares
Wherever we may go,
Therefore I will not, dare not grieve
But rather, calmly say:
"God gave, His will be done since he
Thought best to take away."

O, mothers! when your hearts are sore
Because you had to part
With darlings you were wont to fold
Close, close against your heart,
Weep not in idle, selfish grief,
Let this your comfort be,
The less of earth, the more of Heaven
And immortality.

THE VENTURE.

ON THE DEATH OF A LITTLE CHILD.

Ended is pain's keen anguish,
  Ended Life's tears and grief,
Ended its mortal struggle,
  After a trial brief.

Begun is the life immortal,
  Begun is the angel song,
Begun the joy everlasting
  Which blesses the heavenly throng.

A LESSON FROM THE FLOWERS.

Just as rare buds are opening
  Fully into the light,
We very often see them
  Smitten by sudden blight.

Each petal fades and withers,
  Till of the promised flower
Nothing but dust remaineth
  To prove the spoiler's power.

So often as we journey
  Along life's winding way,

THE VENTURE.

We see rare soul-buds drooping
   In premature decay.

See lovely features stricken
   By Death's relentless hand,
See vacancy where dear ones
   Were wont to sit or stand.

In agony we question
   Why thus the fairest die,
Why thus the joys and pleasures
   Most cherished, soonest fly.

Each flower that fully blossoms,
   Each bud that blighted, dies,
To all our anxious questions
   In chorus clear replies:

"Vainly ye seek endurance
   Upon this sin-stained sphere,
Like peace and full perfection
   It is not here, *not here.*

"Instead, things transitory,
   Probation, trial, flight,
Toil, tears and pain and trouble,
   And daily-coming night.

402526B

THE VENTURE.

"Or blight or rust or mildew
    Wherever you can stray,
Repeat in solemn warning,
    'Passing away, away.'

"Like leaves you bud and flourish,
    Like leaves you fade and fall,
And time's accumulations
    Are heaped above you all."

Evening and noon and morning,
    Each hour, each moment brief,
In a perpetual current
    That mocks all human grief.

The flowing and the ebbing
    Of human life goes on,
Rare soul-buds briefly flourish,
    Droop, fade, and then are *gone*.

Learn then, each precious lesson
    The flowers by voiceless speech
Divinely are commissioned
    Throughout all time to teach.

Obey the voice of reason,
    Be true, be always strong,

THE VENTURE. 101

To struggle with temptation,
  To shun and censure wrong.

Obey the call of Heaven,
  Improve each precious power,
With every sixty minutes
  Construct a *golden hour.*

Pause not in idle dreaming,
  Shrink not in coward fear,
Press on, the blest HEREAFTER
  Repays right action here.

THE OLD GRAVE-DIGGER.

Dig his grave well, men, dig his grave well,
  Many a grave did he dig in his day,
Many a time at the hush of the knell,
  He shouldered his tools and trudged briskly away,
Away to the city where silently dwell
  The young and the aged, the high and the low,
The happy of heart, and the sad, who could tell
  Most pitiful stories of trial and woe.

Fill his grave well, men, fill his grave well,
  Many a grave did he fill in his day,

THE VENTURE.

Many a time when the bitter tears fell
  From eyes of fond mourners, he shoveled away,
Shoveled and patted and pressed down the soil,
  The soft, yielding soil, that hid wholly from sight
Some dear one, some darling, for whom care and toil
  Was pleasure, sweet pleasure, was even delight.

Smooth his grave well, men, smooth his grave well,
  Many a grave did he smooth in his day,
Many a time, as survivors can tell,
  He shaped graves most deftly, and bid sods to lay
Over the form which insatiate Death
  Had touched with its icy, mysterious hand,
Had robbed by one stroke, of volition and breath,
  And laid with the silent, the slain of the land.

SONGS AND HYMNS.

MUSIC ALL AROUND US.

There is music in the sunbeams,
  As in rival speed they stray,
Waking, warming into being
  Things of beauty every day,
Guiding and enriching millions,
  Helping both the false and true,
And exulting at the measure
  Of the good they daily do.

There is music in the breezes
  Which are talking to the trees,
Of their travels over mountains,
  Verdant vales and rocky leas;
While they fan our fevered temples,
  List, they sing a merry song,
And its burden is, "O, mortals,
  Time, like us, moves fast along."

There is music in the lightning,
  When it makes the thunders roar;
There is music in the rain-drops,
  When the clouds their treasures pour,
Every drop is but the echo
  Of some sweet, celestial sound,

THE VENTURE

God has mercifully bidden
  To re-echo o'er the ground.

There is music in our spirits,
  Songs of joy or cries of woe,
Echoed forth in word or actions,
  As the moments from us go.
Aye, within us and around us,
  At all times and everywhere,
There is music, ceaseless thrilling,
  Ringing out upon the air.

A CENTENNIAL HYMN.

God of ages, Head of nations,
  Humbly bowing at thy feet,
We with grateful adoration
  Will thy holy name repeat,
Then in righteous triumph rising,
  We will tell the wondering world
How Thine arm has kept our banner
  For a hundred years unfurled.

Savage tribes have fled before us,
  Fled in fear and wild dismay,
To the wilderness or desert,

THE VENTURE.

Followed close by beasts of prey.
Prairies have become vast cities,
　Forests, fruitful fields and bowers,
Lofty mountains and vast deserts
　Highways strewn with wondrous flowers.

Proudly scorning all oppression,
　Pitying all who are oppressed,
Holding freedom a possession
　Without which no soul is blessed;
Making liberty our goddess,
　Linking close her name with Thine,
We at duty's call have freely
　Measured out life's crimson wine.

With progression for our motto,
　Onward with a steady pace,
Tho' great mountains towered before us,
　Or, on ocean's trackless space
We have pressed, till foes admiring
　Offered the fraternal hand,
Pledging honor and allegiance
　To our laws and to our land.

Where ere while was but a handful,
　Asking mercy, offering praise,

THE VENTURE.

Millions now are proudly gathered,
  Talking of the bygone days,
Joining with triumphant voices,
  And with eyes suffused with tears,
Telling how Thy hand has led us
  Forward for a hundred years.

Grandly speeds along the chorus,
  Wafted by the summer breeze,
Echoed by the hills and valleys,
  Rocks and waters, fields and trees,
Bugles' notes and drums' loud clatter,
  Cannon's boom and musket's roar,
Blending with our myriad voices,
  Sound our triumph o'er and o'er.

Being fully proved, the nation,
  Making Thee its God and Lord,
Will attain the state and station
  Promised in Thy holy word.
Fondly gazing on our banner,
  While all earth and heaven hears,
We commend to Thee our country
  For all coming hundred years.

THE VENTURE.

TO-DAY AND TOMORROW.

If we turn to God to-day,
  Tomorrow may find us re-turning,
And if we trim our lamp of faith,
  Tomorrow may find it burning,
And we can rejoice when the Master's voice
  Praiseth the brilliant burning.

If we do our duty to-day,
  Though hard may be the doing,
Tomorrow shall conscience approve, and we
  Have never a cause for rueing,
But can justly rejoice when the Master's
      voice
  Commendeth our well-doing.

If we bear our cross to-day,
  Though hard may be the bearing,
Tomorrow the cross may be changed for the
      crown,
  And our freed soul may be sharing
The rest that is found in Heaven above,
  Whither we are now repairing.

THE VENTURE. 109

GOD IS GOOD AND GOD IS LOVE.

When the warm life-tide is flowing
  Through our veins with steady speed,
When no adverse winds are blowing,
  And the mind from care is freed,
'When the path lies straight before us,
  And our sky is bright above,
Then we sing in joyful chorus:
  "God is good, and God is love."

When stern pain with tortures ready,
  Takes its place within the frame,
And life's tide, that once was steady,
  Floweth like a fitful flame,
When the path grows rough and winding,
  And the clouds are black above,
Tho' the tears our eyes are blinding,
  Still we murmur, "God is love."

But when those we fondly trusted
  Prove us false and wound us sore,
When we know a cross of anguish
  We must bear till life is o'er,
Then we center our affections
  Upon things which are above,

110 *THE VENTURE.*

And convinced by calm reflections,
Sing the chorus, "God is love."

THE STILLING OF THE TEMPEST.

Wildly the storm tossed fair Galilee's waters,
Loudly the thunder-bolts echoed and rolled,
Swiftly the lightning flashed hither and thither,
Voyagers filling with terror untold.

And long as Jesus lay peacefully sleeping,
Vainly his followers steered for the shore,
Vainly they cried, "Master, save us, we perish!"
Or prayed that the storm would its fury give o'er.

But when He woke, and in majesty rising,
Bade the wild tumult of Nature "Be still!"
Quickly a peace that was wholly surprising
Proved how *divine* were His words and His will.

Time is a sea, and as ships we are sailing,
Onward and outward, day after day,
Tempests within and around us prevailing,
Hasten to wreck us, wherever our way.

And we grow faint, and would certainly perish,
Did not that voice which gave Galilee peace

THE VENTURE. 111

Bid each wild tempest which we must encounter
　Quickly its menacing fury to cease.

Oh, perfect, Oh, sweet is the calm that succeedeth
　Each tempest which Jesus commands to be still!
And pleasant indeed are the paths where He leadeth
　Each soul that relies on His wisdom and will.

With Him in the vessel, or sleeping or waking,
　We steer for our harbor, our haven above,
Secure, since each trial or danger o'ertaking
　Must yield, as of old, to His power and His love.

A SONG OF EXULTATION.

A Saviour, a Saviour! Proclaim the glad tidings,
　Resound it afar through earth's spacoius domain,
Till each echo that now is in silence abiding
　Has caught and re-echoed the wonderful strain;
Till every soul wending earth's ways, sadly bending
　Beneath heavy crosses of suffering and sin,
Hears, and in humble, implicit confiding,
　Hastens its part of the theme to begin.

A Saviour, a Saviour! No longer in anguish
　We sadly must languish, o'erburdened with guilt,

112   *THE VENTURE.*

A ransom was offered, a sacrifice proffered,
   The blood of the sinless for sinners was spilt;
The mountains have rended, the victims ascended,
   The sword sharp for vengeance in its scabbard is
      laid,
We, freely forgiven, accepted of Heaven,
   No longer by fear or by doubt are dismayed.

A Saviour, a Saviour! now graciously pleading,
   For us interceding, with tenderest love,
Urging humanity for moral fraility,
   Sharing our sorrows, his pity to prove;
With us abiding and tenderly chiding,
   Wherever we wonder away from the way;
Guarding and guiding, and never deriding
   Though from his love we rebelliously stray.

A Saviour, a Saviour! with awe we adore him,
   And bow at his name with exultant accord,
Our homage we offer, our services proffer,
   And gratefully claim Him our Master, our Lord,
His kind mediation secures our salvation,
   And we of the law are no longer afraid;
No grace he denies us, but freely supplies us,
   So long as on Him our affections are stayed.

THE VENTURE.

A Saviour, a Saviour! Oh, mortals, receive Him,
  Own Him your Messiah, Redeemer and King,
With cherubs and seraphs and highest arch-angels,
  Unite in glad concert, His praises to sing.
His cross high upholding, his glory unfolding,
  Inspired by his wonderful mercy and love,
In meek adoration, with devout exultation,
  Press on till ye view Him in glory above.

A REQUEST.

O, friend, when thinking for me to pray,
  At morning, at noon-tide, or closing of day,
Pray not that the treasures of earth may be mine,
  That my sun of prosperity always may shine;
Pray not that my path may be constantly straight,
  That foes ne'er confront me in anger or hate;
Pray not that no sorrow my heart ever try,
  Nor the hopes that I cherish ne'er wither or die.

But pray that Our Father, the bounteous God,
  Who mingles the cup and proportions the rod,
In mercy will give me true wisdom of mind,
  And generous heart-wealth, so nicely combined,
That whether my portion be weal or be woe,
  So long as He wills, I a pilgrim shall go,

114   THE VENTURE.

I may ever discern and keep closely in view
    The wrong from the right and the false from the
        true.

For wisdom and heart-wealth are treasures that
        bless,
    When gold has no power any wrong to redress,
Of the kingdom of God they are parcel and part,
    And are free for the poor and the lowly in heart,
And they live when the treasures of earth are
        decayed,
    When the form in the grave for long ages has laid.
Then pray not that the treasures of earth may be
        mine,
    But that wisdom and heart-wealth within me
        combine.

          ————

        A THANKSGIVING HYMN.

Thanksgiving and the voice of melody,
    These are the sounds which best become us,
        when
The harvest fills our garners plenteously,
    And peace and comfort in our dwellings reign.

Thanksgiving blent with humble, grateful prayer,
    .These are the tributes which we justly owe,

THE VENTURE.

As the recipients of the tender care
  Our Father doth so constantly bestow.

Thanksgiving, adoration, love and praise,
  These are the offerings which we meekly bring
Now that another year has told its days,
  And paid its tithes to the Eternal King.

Father Supreme! deign to accept thy due,
  Of praise, thanksgiving and adoring love,
For mercies past, and still with blessings strew
  Our paths, as onward through the years we
    move.

A DOLLAR OR TWO.

Of all the tunes to which we move
  As through this world we ceaseless rove,
There is one tune which guides and sways
  Us onward in our devious ways,
And half the things we say or do
  Are to that tune, "a dollar or two."

"A dollar or two" among our friends
  To this same tune our friendship bends,
From honest worth we coldly turn,
  Its proffered friendship proudly spurn,

THE VENTURE.

And try to think that false is true,
  When gilt by dollars, one or two.

The merchant, when to him we go,
  Will scan us o'er from crown to toe,
And having weighed us in his scale
  Of cents and dollars, if we fail
Of dollars, with indifference,
  He shows us goods worth only cents.

But while he weighs us, should we rise
  To dollars, he will not disguise,
His pleasure, but with gracious air,
  To please us he no pains will spare,
And then, to prove his pleasure true,
  Discounts a dollar, one or two.

The lawyer pleads his client's cause,
  Not to the tune of righteous laws,
But by the purse each client holds,
  And by the coin which each enfolds,
And proves his case alone is true
  Who shows most dollars, one or two.

The doctor, too, doth come and go
  To us in times of pain and woe,
And deals his pills and potions out

THE VENTURE.

The while his learning he doth spout,
In measures many, large or few,
  As we have dollars, one or two.

Whoe'er we be, where'er we go,
  Whate'er our cause for joy or woe,
Our state is fixed, our doom is sealed,
  By law which seldom is repealed,
And we find favors, great or few,
  As we have dollars, one or two.

Yet there is joy for us, for though
  To this base tune awhile we go,
There comes a time, a glorious day,
  When love of wealth shall pass away,
And we will not, in all we do,
  Be judged by dollars, one or two,

COUNT THE COST.

Often while we are journeying
  Life's mazy turnings through,
Thinking, proposing, planning,
  What and how we will do,
If we would pause a moment,
  Calmly to count the cost,

THE VENTURE.

Much labor might be treasured
  That now is wholly lost.

Or when we are arranging
  Where and when we will go,
And how our independence
  To others we will show,
If we would pause a moment,
  Calmly to count the cost,
Much honor might be treasured
  That now is wholly lost.

And oft when meditating
  Of words which we will speak,
To thrill another's bosom,
  Or tinge another's cheek,
If we would pause a moment,
  Calmly to count the cost,
Much life-breath might be treasured
  That now is wholly lost.

Therefore let us be watchful,
  And careful every hour,
Remembering words and actions
  Are things of mighty power,
And always in our planning
  That nothing may be lost,

THE VENTURE. 119

In profit, peace and pleasure,
Count carefully the cost.

WHEN WE FORGIVE.

When real or fancied wrong has stung
The hearts that should in love abide,
When hate its galling taunts has flung
Till anger for revenge has cried,
The surest power to break the spell
And waken love where love should live,
Or ring revenge its burial knell,
Is the entreating word, "Forgive."

"Forgive!" it is the bravest word
That human lips can ever speak,
And nature's heights and depths are stirred
When men of men forgiveness seek,
Legions of angels hover near
To bear the tidings up to Heaven,
When to the plea, "Forgive," they hear
The generous answer, "All's forgiven."

"Forgive!" O, if we would forgive
As oft we pray to be forgiven,
We then would prove it sweet to live,
And make our earth another Heaven,

THE VENTURE.

Anger and malice, pride and hate,
And every sin o'er which we pray,
Would at the contrite word "Forgive,"
In dire confusioh haste away.

CHORUS.—"Forgive," it moves the heart of God,
"Forgive," it stays the chastening rod,
And we fortaste the joys of Heaven
When we forgive and are forgiven.

"LAND AHEAD."

"Land ahead," the mariner singeth,
As his vessel ploughs the deep,
And his words like music ringeth,
Rousing dreamers from their sleep.

Fellow-mariner o'er Time's ocean,
Though thy course tempestous be,
Though 'mid trouble's wild commotion
Hope is nearly gone from thee;

Though no light thou now discernest,
Nor a haven wherein to rest,
Though the calm for which thou yearnest
Seldom here may fill thy breast;

THE VENTURE.

There is land ahead, though never
  Mortal eyes its shores have seen,
A sure haven where anchors never
  Slip, nor breakers intervene.

There is light forever beaming
  From the glorious other side,
And with full effulgence streaming
  Far across Time's stormy tide.

There is rest and joyful singing,
  In the presence of our God,
Shouts of gladness often ringing
  Through His glorious abode,

Land and light and rest and gladness
  Thou than this can ask no more,
Why then live in gloomy sadness,
  When life's storms will soon be o'er?

BEAR AND FORBEAR.

This world is full of pain and trouble,
  This world is full of grief and care,
But though our portion may be double,
  We still should meekly bravely, bear.

THE VENTURE.

This world is full of pride and scorning,
  And spiteful foes who will not spare,
Yet still there comes the gentle warning,
  The counsel, "Patiently forbear."

And he is wise who while forbearing,
  And meekly sparing, thinks and sings,
And speaks in words of calm comparing
  Of what we reckon "better things."

Therefore if you would truly know
  Life is worth living and would share
Heaven's blessedness where'er you go,
  Make this your rule, "Bear and forbear."

TRY TO BE HAPPY.

Try to be happy, 'tis wiser and better,
  Always to look on the pleasantest side,
Than to turn doubter, desponder or fretter,
  Thinking more evil will surely betide;
Fearing the sun will not shine on the morrow,
  Or that the breezes adversely will blow;
Friends all forsake us and trouble and sorrow
  Track and precede us wherever we go.

THE VENTURE.

CHORUS.—Try to be happy, try to be happy,
  Try to be happy to-day,
  Try to be happy to-day and tomorrow,
  Try to be happy alway.

Try to be happy, 'twill profit you never
  To worry and fret o'er events that are past,
Let all unpleasantness now and forever
  In the deep sea of forgiveness be cast,
Suffer not hatred nor envy nor malice
  That trio of tyrants, to rule in thy heart,
Try to be happy till they and their helpers
  Confused and confounded, wholly depart.

  CHORUS.—

Try to be happy, if pain is distressing,
Thank the Good Father that bad is not worse,
  Time may reveal that a glorious blessing
Waits where you fear are but chances adverse ;
  Light may be shining tomorrow in places
Where you see only dread darkness to-day,
  And you may find that the noblest graces
Grow while the fondest hopes wither away.

  CHORUS.—

THE VENTURE.

Try to be happy, whatever your station,
Struggle and battle with doubt and despair,
There's scarcely a place or a face in creation
But has some feature attractive and fair;
Often reflect and as often remember
That if the sun were to shine all the while,
Nature would weary and May and December
Never would bring us a reason to smile.

    CHORUS.—.

Try to be happy. God rules and is reigning,
Reigning triumphant o'er sea and o'er land,
Grieve him no longer by thankless complaining,
Kiss with submission his chastening hand.
Keep on life's sunny side, questioning never
Why and for what all this trouble and care,
Say "Not as I will," and then you will ever
Offer the wisest and noblest prayer.

    CHORUS.—

WHEN SHALL WE MEET AGAIN?

When shall we meet again?
When shall we greet again?
When shall our voices commingling sound?

THE VENTURE.

When will our path of life
Where lies our toil and strife
To the same centre again circle round?

We may not meet again,
We may not greet again,
Life is uncertain and time full of change,
And hearts here united
In friendship oft plighted,
Distance and circumstance widely estrange.

Yet we shall meet again,
And we shall greet again,
There is a day and an hour yet to come
When our paths now diverging
To one centre emerging
Will leave us rejoicing in Heaven at home.

There when we meet again,
There when we greet again,
Joy like a stream unobstructed will flow,
And the friendships here plighted
Again re-united
Shall in perfection eternally grow.

126   *THE VENTURE.*

TRUTH SHALL TRIUMPH.

"Truth crushed to earth shall rise again,
   The eternal years of God are hers,"
So sang the poet, and his notes
   Each justice-loving spirit stirs
With rapturous joy—though for a while
   Wrong with proud arrogance holds sway,
Its dawn is sure; Truth will arise,
   And go in triumph on her way.

"Truth crushed to earth shall rise again,"
   O, blessed, O, soul-nerving thought!
It dries the tears in many eyes,
   And strengthens hands which long have wrought
Against vast odds of wealth and pride,
   Of selfishness and cruel hate,
Of avarice that planned and tried
   By fraud to raise its own estate.

"Truth crushed to earth shall rise again,"
   Thank God, this promise will abide
Till wrong is vanquished; and all those
   Who Truth and Right have dared deride,
Shall stand aghast to see their work
   Flying as chaff before the wind,

THE VENTURE. 127

And learn as ages onward roll,
How in opposing Truth, they sinned.

"Truth crushed to earth shall rise again,"
Ye friends of justice, hear and heed
This glorious thought, and let it nerve
You when you strength and courage need.
Though multitudes unite to crush,
Hide, baffle, or annihilate,
Truth, cling to her, she will arise
To reign in more than regal state.

LIGHTS ALONG THE SHORE.

When streams are deep and skies are, drear
And fiercely blows the gale.
Till doeful doubt and awful fear
O'er trust and hope prevail,
When courage fails us and we seem
Lost, wrecked forevermore,
What joy intense to catch the gleam
Of lights along the shore!

CHORUS.—O, beauteous lights along the shore!
Or stars or beacons fair,
We bless your beams and yield no more
To billows nor despair.

THE VENTURE.

And oftener still, as on we go,
   Over the sea of Life,
When storms of trial round us blow,
   And shriek in hurried strife;
When hope grows feeble and we deem
   It vain to struggle more,
How cheering to behold a gleam
   Of light from some safe shore!

CHORUS.—

Oh, blessed lights along the shore!
   Telling of coming aid,
Shouting above the tempest's roar,
   "Courage, be not dismayed!"
Soon trial will no more distress,
   Soon suffering will be past,
God will His faithful children bless,
   And shelter from the blast.

CHORUS.—

Oh, friends, as long as on the stream
   Of Life and Time you toss,
Though fierce the gales of trial seem,
   And terrible your loss,
Pause not in terror nor despair,

THE VENTURE. 129

Trust on till life is o'er,
Lo! ever shining brightly fair,
Lights on the Heavenly shore.

CHORUS.—

Oh, glorious lights that flash afar
Sweet messages of love!
That shout above earth's din and jar,
"There's rest and peace above,"
Though storms be long and streams be deep,
Faith, hope, ne'er, ne'er give o'er,
Almighty power will ever keep
Lights on the heavenly shore.

CHORUS.—

THE AGED CHRISTIAN'S TESTIMONY.

I am waiting, calmly waiting,
I am waiting every day
For my passport to that country
Skeptics think so far away,
To that blessed Heavenly Canaan
Where all those by Christ declared
"Heirs of God," receive the "great things"
By almighty love prepared.

THE VENTURE.

Time has brought me grievous trouble,
  Perplexity and loss,
And I often slipped and faltered,
  While alone I bear my cross.
But upon the Rock of Ages
  I at last my burden laid,
And He proved a strong deliverer,
  Loving shelter, guide and aid.

Now my pilgrimage is closing,
  All my labors are complete,
Fast the sands of time are slipping
  From beneath my feeble feet,
But with calm, submissive spirit,
  Steadfast faith and purest love,
I am waiting for my passport
  To the better world above.

GOD AND OURSELVES.

We doubt His love for many an hour,
  We set a limit to His power;
Question the wisdom of His way,
  His laws with boldness disobey,
      Yet He doth spare,
      And still forbear,

THE VENTURE. 131

And grant us all a generous share
Of sun and shade and sky and air.

We lay each other in the scales
Of our own judgment, and who fails,
Of our set weight, of them we say,
They wander in a godless way,
Yet He doth spare,
And still forbear,
And grant to all a generous share
Of sun and shade and sky and air.

And even tho' He doth commend,
We grudge our cavilings to end,
And when his voice commandeth, "peace,"
Reluctantly our strivings cease,
Yet He doth spare,
And still forbear,
And grant to all a generous share
Of sun and shade and sky and air.

Because He sees each human heart,
And knows the struggle and the smart
Which each must pass before the goal
Is gained, where body parts with soul,
So He doth spare,
And still forbear,

THE VENTURE.

And grant to all a generous share
In His impartial Father care.

A WEDDING–DAY SONG.

Ring, wedding-bells! Ring loud and clear,
  Sweet notes of hearty gladness,
Ring, and a truce to doubt and fear,
  And every form of sadness.

Ring, sweetly ring! till every ear
  That feels your glad vibrations
Thrills joyfully and waits to hear
  Your further revelations.

Ring out your tenderest, purest strain,
  For holy troth is plighted,
And they who moved ere while as twain,
  As one are now united.

Ring out your loftiest praise of hope,
  And noble aspiration,
For hopes long cherished find to-day
  A happy consumation.

Ring, sweetly ring! until all hearts
  To love now growing strangers,

THE VENTURE. 133

R new their youth, rehearse their parts,
And flee all faithless dangers.

Ring, till your peals reach all the zones,
And no one dares disparage
Society's best corner-stone,
True, virtuous love and marriage.

MAKE FLOWERS YOUR FRIENDS.

In the sunny days of childhood,
When your heart is light and gay,
And earth seems a fairy wildwood,
Where you may unhindered stray,
That your soul may carry beauty
Everywhere your pathway tends,
And your heart be strong for duty,
Make the flowers your daily friends.

When the joys of childhood vanish,
And your life is in its prime,
When more weighty thoughts have banished
Many a youthful thought and rhyme,
That they may return to cheer you,
When your heart with sorrow bends,
And that angels may seem near you,
Make the lovely flowers your friends.

THE VENTURE.

When life's spring and summer sweetness
　Have to autumn ripeness grown,
When the hope of joy's completeness
　From your heart has wholly flown,
Lest you doubt the love enduring
　That to all your needs attends,
And grow thankless or desponding,
　Make the fragrant flowers your friends.

They will talk to you of power,
　Power deep and high and wide,
Wisdom, love and tender mercy,
　They will image, side by side;
They will speak of dew and sunlight,
　And each thing which nature blends,
To produce them, and forever
　They will be your faithful friends.

REFLECTIONS AFTER READING THE FORTY-SIXTH PSALM.

"God is our refuge," when a gale
　Of trouble round us wildly blows,
Till hope and faith and courage fail,
　And we, reviled by cruel foes,
Eagerly look for some safe place

THE VENTURE.

Wherein to hide from foe and storm,
Oh, then the thought is grandly sweet,
God is our refuge and retreat.

God is our strength when pain and grief
Have tortured us till strength is gone,
And life appears a dismal night,
Without a star, without a dawn,
Then like a sunbeam, warm and clear,
Dispelling all our doubt and gloom,
Gilding our pathway's breadth and length,
Comes the blest thought, God is our strength.

God is our very present help,
In time of trouble and of need,
Oh, blessed anchor for our trust,
Oh, safe foundation for our creed.
Let toil, perplexity and pain
Heart-ache and tears our portion prove,
All will but make us more and more
Our Refuge, Strength and Help adore.

WE NEED NOT SIT WITH FOLDED HANDS.

Though we may not cross the oceans,
Nor climb the mountains high,

THE VENTURE.

Though we can not feed the thousands
   Who for bread in anguish cry,
Though we have not gold and silver
   To bestow with lavish hand,
Nor the power to build a structure
   That would beautify the land,

We need not sit down with folded hands,
   To sigh the hours away,
Scorning all the little duties
   Which within and round us lay;
Keeping from the humble vineyards
   And the fields for harvest white,
Ever beckoning us to labor
   Zealously for Truth and Right;

Calling us to warn the erring,
   And to comfort those who weep;
Bidding us to help the straying,
   Virtue's holy paths to keep;
Urging us to scatter broadcast
   Kindly words and loving deeds,
Meanwhile sedulously guarding
   Our own hearts from sinful weeds.

Every moment brings some duty,
   And if we that duty do,

THE VENTURE.

In the blessed, long forever,
  We our course will never rue,
But like some brave victor looking
  O'er a battle-field well won,
We with honest joy can listen
  To the Master's pleased "Well done."

For as Time is made of seconds,
  Earth of minute grains of sand,
So the doing little duties
  · Tinges life with colors grand,
Stamps the character with beauty,
  And enwreaths around the name
God's approval, far more lasting
  Than the laurel wreath of fame.

HERE AND THERE.

Here the solemn, utter silence,
  And the lonely isolation,
Here the mourning o'er desires
  That can have no consummation,
Here the curses and the losses,
  And the weary, weary pain,
And the longings for dear faces
  Life will show us not again.

THE VENTURE.

There the music, sweet and thrilling,
  And the countless, happy throng,
There the knowledge that desires
  Which were here denied, were wrong,
There the crowns and harps all golden,
  And the satisfying rest,
And the joy with which the ransomed
  Shall forever more be blest.

TRUST IN THE LORD ALWAYS.

"Trust ye in the Lord forever, for in the Lord Jehovah
is everlasting strength."—Isiah xxvi., 4.

In youth's bright morn, in life's full prime,
  Where'er thy path may tend,
Trust in the Lord, and all the time
  Make Him thy guide and friend.
If joys along thy pathway teem,
  Or not a joy remains,
Still trust, long as life's crimson stream
  Flows warmly in thy veins.

Trust in the Lord when prime is past,
  And the white seals of age
Are fixed upon thee, firm and fast,
  Till thou no more canst wage

THE VENTURE. 139

Life's battle as in younger days,
   Then firmly trust the Lord,
Commit to Him all, all thy ways,
   And rest upon His word.

Trust in the Lord when Death's cold hand
   Touches thy quivering heart,
When Life's warm stream is at a stand
   And soul and flesh must part.
What we call death is only *change*,
   The spirit's second birth,
Its freedom evermore to range,
   Free from the ills of earth.

Then trust the Lord in youth and joy,
   Trust him in age and pain,
Earth's mightiest powers can not destroy
   If He thy cause maintain.
Oh, then, trust him implicitly,
   Though short or long life's length,
For in Jehovah, Lord of all,
   Is everlasting strength.

THE WILL OF GOD.

"God's will be done," if we would say this meekly
   When by pretended friends the heart is stung,

THE VENTURE.

When some bright star of hope we long have followed
 Is like a metor from its orbit flung,
We then would find we have a friend unfailing,
 To sympathize, to cheer, to guide and save,
A star that o'er all darkening powers prevailing,
 Will light us safely, even through the grave.

"God's will be done." If we would say this meekly,
 When pain is torturing us with ruthless hand,
When sore bereavement, bitter grief and sorrow
 Pursue us like a savage, murderous band,
We then would find wisdom and love commanding
 Our every pang—and calmly keeping still,
The peace which passeth skeptics' understanding,
 Deep as the ocean, would our spirits fill.

"God's will be done." If we would say it meekly,
 When called to bear some heavy, worldly loss,
Some strong perplexity or care or trouble,
 That to our judgment seems a needless cross,
We then would see experiences we blindly
 Regard as evils, and as such deplore,
Is discipline, arranged with purpose kindly,
 By Him whose love and wisdom we ignore.

"God's will be done." Forever it is wisest
 Forever it is kindest, truest, best,

THE VENTURE. 141

Forever it insures most present blessing,
  Most future satisfaction, peace and rest.
The sun may cease to shine, the moon be darkened,
  The stars may fall, the solid rocks decay,
But if we to God's word have humbly hearkened,
  We shall have light and blessedness alway.

A SONG SUGGESTED BY A SONG.

"The last rose of summer," a fair maiden sang,
And her voice like the echoes of fairy bells rang,
  "The last rose of summer," Oh, sad is the day
When the queen of the flowers is fading away.

In springtime, when roses abundantly bloom,
We thoughtlessly pluck them, inhale their perfume,
  Dissect their rich petals and toss them around,
Or carelessly trample them into the ground.

But when every rosebud is blasted or flown,
And the last one is blooming alone, all alone,
  We think it of blossoms most fragrant and fair,
And pluck it with almost a reverent air.

My life has its roses, yet sometimes a thorn
Of misunderstanding, of pride or of scorn,

142 *THE VENTURE.*

Has pierced me and mentally caused me to say,
"My last rose of summer" is fading away.

But just as the roses exhale sweet perfume,
Tho' plucked, nevermore in bright beauty to bloom,
So I must be patient, forbearing and kind,
And with balm of forgiveness heart-bruises must
bind.

Because the same power that bids them decay
For me writes the sentence sure, "passing away,"
And as they yield fragrance when beauty is fled,
So I would leave kind thoughts when laid with the
dead.

"The last rose of summer" to-day is my song,
And the lessons it teaches are many and long,
Oh, wretched and much to be pitied are they
Whose last rose of summer has faded away.

NOTHING IS LOST.

No seed is lost, though long it lie,
Deep hidden in the soil,
Or if unnourished it may die,
Despite the sower's toil,
It is not lost although in ne'er

THE VENTURE. 143

In beauteous verdure spring,
As grain of dust, 'twill help to rear
Some other seed or thing.

CHORUS.—No seed shall die, nothing be lost,
No influence lose its power,
The seed shall change, the lost be found
In some propitious hour.

Oh, cheering thought! each little seed
We late or early sow,
Tho' it be destined or decreed
Never to sprout or grow,
To leaf nor luscious fruit nor flower,
Nor precious, golden grain,
Some thing will prove some future hour,
We sowed it not in vain.

CHORUS.—

Oh, blessed joy-inspiring thought!
Not one material thing
Is wholly lost—one's poverty
To others wealth may bring,
For compensation is a law
Fixed by almighty power,

THE VENTURE.

And granite rocks may grow from seed
  Too weak to bear a flower.

  CHORUS.—

Nothing is lost, our words and deeds
  Which seem to lack in power,
For good or ill, are fruitful seeds
  Awaiting but their hour,
Their favoring circumstance or time
  In which to grow and bloom,
And help some soul to God and heaven,
  Or speed it to its doom.

  CHORUS.—

For influence is a mighty wave,
  Forever rolling on,
On through all time tho' to the grave
  Mortality be gone,
And onward it shall ever roll,
  Despite all human skill,
Exerting upon many a soul
  Some power for good or ill.

Oh, solemn, wholly solemn thought!
  Our influence is a power,

THE VENTURE.   145

Mighty, tho' subtle, and is fraught
  With issues every hour,
For good or ill, for weal or woe,
  From dawn till set of sun,
Whate'er our state, where'er we go,
  Outward the currents run.

CHORUS.—

THE VOYAGE OF LIFE.

While across time's ocean sailing,
  Should thy sky adversely lower,
And temptation's waves assailing
  Rock thee with alarming power,
When thy faith begins to waver,
  And thy strength and hope grow small,
Raise thine arms to Heaven, where Jesus
  Waits to heed thy faintest call.

Should thy friends most loved and cherished
  All desert or wound thee sore,
And fond hopes like snow-flakes perished,
  Cheer thy spirit nevermore,
When thy heart is sick with trouble,
  And thy mind dark with despair,

THE VENTURE.

Look to Jesus, who regards thee
   With the tenderest love and care.

All regardless of derision,
   Whatsoever may befall,
Though all tear-dimmed be thy vision,
   And fresh trials may appal, .
Long as life's voyage is tending
   Outward, nearer to its end,
Look to Jesus, He will prove thee
   An unfailing, precious friend.

CHORUS.—Look to Jesus! Look to Jesus!
     Whatsoe'er thy trouble be,
    Trust in Jesus! Trust in Jesus!
     He will prove a friend to thee.

SWEET MEMORY BELLS.

Sweet memory bells, ring out your chimes,
   Recall the hours forever fled,
Recount to us those happy times
   When hope o'er life rich halo shed,
When hearts were tender, trusting, true,
   Unchilled by disappointment's blast,
And all the hours too swiftly flew,
   To swell the cycles of the Past.

THE VENTURE. 147

Sweet memory bells! ring, softly ring,
　Bring back to us those happy years
When we could gaily smile and sing
　And found small cause for sighs or tears;
When we were bound by many cords
　To life, and all that makes life dear,
And sought by kindly, hopeful words
　Less happy souls to light and cheer.

Ring out your chimes until again
　The faith, the trust of childhood come,
And we can realize all men
　Are brothers, seeking for one home;
Ring, until envy, malice, hate
　Are banished from our hearts awhile,
And we with peace, with joy elate,
　Exult in God's approving smile.

Oh, ring, in your own magic way,
　Until the present seems the past,
Until the troubles of to-day
　In deep oblivion's sea are cast,
Until the tears that dim our eyes
　Are changed to smiles o'er joys long fled,
And we roam free 'neath cloudless skies
　Clasping the hands of loved ones dead.

THE VENTURE.

Ring clear, ring loud, the echoing cries
　　Of thwarted hopes have dulled our ears,
And time from us exacts so much
　　While swelling the eternal years,
Ring, softly ring, until your peal
　　Awakes some long-forgotten song,
Over each wearied sense to steal
　　Like voices loved but silent long,

Ring, ring, until we cease all groans
　　O'er joys created but to fly,
Until we hush regretful moans.
　　O'er flowers we cherished but to die,
Ring, till our shrinking souls grow strong
　　Bravely to bear our Heaven-shaped cross,
With patience, tho' life may seem long
　　Or rough with trouble, pain or loss.

NOT FOREVER.

Not forever shall we sorrow,
　　Not forever shall we sigh,
Not forever shall our future
　　Closely wrapped in mystery lie,
Not forever shall we wander,
　　Feeling desolate and lone,

THE VENTURE.

149

Feeling that among earth's millions
　We are friendless and unknown.

Sometime we shall cease to sorrow,
　Sometime we shall cease to sigh,
Sometime darkness will have vanished
　Wholly from our spirit's sky,
We no more shall sadly wander,
　Desolate and drear and lone,
But among a happy people,
　Knowing all we shall be known.

Even now the hours are flying,
And the darkness fades away,
　Even now we catch the glimmer
Of the promised "sometime" day.
　Faith looks up with exultation,
Hope begins the cheering song,
　"Not forever shall we sorrow,
Sometime speedeth fast along."

ASK ME NOT TO DRINK.

Oh, ask me not to sip the wine,
　The sparkling, ruby wine,
For though within the goblet bright

THE VENTURE.

It harmlessly may shine,
A horrid spell, a fatal charm
Unseen is lurking there,
Which, if they once but touch the soul,
Will lure it to despair.

Oh, tempt me not to taste the wine,
The sparkling, ruby wine,
For though within the goblet bright
It harmlessly may shine,
In every drop a serpent lurks,
To sting the trusting heart,
And lure it from all lovely things
Forevermore to part.

Oh, urge me not to drink the wine,
The sparkling, ruby wine,
For though within the goblet bright
It harmlessly may shine,
It holds a flame to wrap the life
In more than midnight gloom,
And set upon the precious soul
The seal of hopeless doom.

I dare not, will not sip the wine,
The sparkling, ruby wine,
For though within the goblet bright

THE VENTURE. 151

It harmlessly may shine,
If I should sip the treach'rous draught,
A brother or a friend
Might be thereby induced to drink,
And ruin be the end.

CHORUS.—Oh, ask me not, Oh, tempt me not
To sip the sparkling wine,
For, left within the goblet bright,
It harmlessly may shine.

A SONG FOR "THE MAKE HOME HAPPY" ARMY.

All around us there is sorrow,
Toil and pain and grief and woe,
Weary, troubled looks confront us,
Almost everywhere we go,
And to cheer the sad and weary
In each home throughout our land,
We have joined ourselves together
As a "Make home happy" band.

CHORUS.—"Make home happy, make home happy,"
Is our motto every day,
"Make home happy, make home happy,"
While we work and while we play.

THE VENTURE.

From the fertile western prairies
  From the rugged northern hills,
From the verdant southern valleys,
  Through which flow the noisy rills,
We have gathered, and have promised,
  Heart to heart and hand to hand,
We will try, *all try* to scatter
  Happiness throughout the land.

CHORUS.—

Lo, our weapons—they are mighty,
  Though not made of iron or steel,
And will make the hosts of trouble
  From their strongholds quickly reel,
Love we carry as our rifle,
  Of a sure, unerring aim,
While kind *Charity*, our sabre,
  Is already known to fame.

Hark! our battle-trump is calling,
  For recruits through all the land,
Hark! the bugle-notes of duty
  Clearly echo its command,
Brothers, sisters, haste to join us,
  And our doctrine daily test,

THE VENTURE. 153

That by making others happy,
  We with happiness are blest.

CHORUS.—

LOVE AND FLOWERS.

One day I passed a garden,
  And my love was there,
With her hands brim-full of flowers,
  Of flowers sweet and rare.
But sweeter than the flowers,
  From vine or shrub or tree,
As she stood there in the garden,
  Seemed my love to me,

I stopped to see the flowers,
  The flowers sweet and rare,
And I said, "they all are beautiful,
  Are beautiful and rare."
She blushingly assented,
  And I could plainly see
As we stood there in the garden,
  That my love loved me.

Then I grew bold to tell her,
  To tell her that my heart

THE VENTURE.

Held her, of flowers and treasures
  The fairest, richest part,
And when I paused and waited
  An answering word or sign,
She proffered me the flowers,
  And softly whispered, "Thine."

We have walked in many gardens,
  Since then, my love and I,
We have seen our hopes, like flowers,
  Droop and wither, fade and die.
But we never have regretted
  What we said that happy day,
When our hands were full of flowers,
  Full of flowers, sweet and gay.

For though we met with trials,
  We invariably have found
Thorns grow among the roses,
  On the best attended ground.
Yet each trouble and each trial
  Has a purpose or a use,
And the roses are the sweetest
  Where the thorns are most profuse.

THE VENTURE. 155

THE FIRST ALARM.

Fire! fire! hark, the echo
    Falls upon the autumn air,
Plainly saying there is danger
    And a cause for watchful care.
But the cry is now so common
    That we have no cause to fear,
In a little while the danger
    Will entirely disappear.

CHORUS.—Fire! Fire! Fire! Fire!
        Yet we have no cause to fear,
        Water, water quenches ever,
    Lake and river both are near.

Fire! Fire! hark, more quickly
    Sounds afar the awful cry,
Lurid flames are leaping upward,
    As if they would touch the sky.
But we need not fear nor tremble,
    For the city's heart is strong,
And before the flames can reach it,
    They must struggle hard and long.

CHORUS.—

THE VENTURE.

Fire! Fire! louder, clearer,
  Bursts the sound from many bells,
Every peal and every echo,
  Of increasing danger tells,
But there is no lack of water,
  And the flames e're long must yield,
We for years have dwelt securely,
  And are masters of the field.

    CHORUS.—

THE CONFLAGRATION.

Fire! Fire! Fire! Fire!
  Hark! with awful force and speed
From the bells the words are leaping,
  Saying there is fire indeed,
Saying water, mighty water,
  Has not stopped its onward course,
And the flames are rushing forward
  Scorning every human force.

CHORUS.—Fire! Fire! Fire! Fire!
  Fire upon every side,
    Heaven help us, Heaven save us
  From the awful, threatening tide.

THE VENTURE. 157

Fire! Fire! Fire! Fire!
  Hope within us almost dies,
Awful fear and consternation
  Shows in many tones and eyes,
Precious homes and hopes are burning,
  Toils of many a weary year;
Fire to dust and smoke is turning
  Everything the heart holds dear.

CHORUS.—

Fire! Fire! Fire! Fire!
  Hark, the word rings yet more clear,
Onward sweeps the burning current,
  The proud city's heart anear;
Faster, faster every moment
  Rushes on the glowing tide,
Scattering blackened desolation
  Want and woe on every side.

CHORUS.—

Lo! the city's heart is burning,
  Melting to its very core,
All it claimed of life and beauty
  Is forever past and o'er;
Ruins and small heaps of ashes

158 *THE VENTURE.*

Tell alone of what has been
Once the joy, the pride, the glory
Of ten thousand busy men.

CHORUS.—

Fire! Fire! Fire! Fire!
Long ago the echo died,
But with some of us who heard it,
It forever will abide,
And as pilgrims to their Mecca,
We will often sadly turn
To the city's core and center,
Which was builded but to burn.

CHORUS.—

MISCELLANEOUS POEMS.

THE VENTURE. 161

THE WORTH OF PRAYER.

The power, the worth of prayer, how vastly great,
  Transcending all earth's powers to help or bless,
Making the dreariest spot, the hardest fate
  In seeming but a very little less
Than a clear vision or foretaste of Heaven,
  For steadfast faith's perpetuation given.

Look to the past, the mighty, vanished past,
  Hark to the marvelous stories it can tell,
Of rocks and skies holding their treasures fast,
  Of fire that from the heavens quickly fell,
When some old prophet, to attain an end,
  Prayed water might be stayed or fire descend.

Look to that brother, who by fraud had won
  The birthright from his tired, despairing twin,
When years their stern, instructive work had done,
  And he, full conscious of his selfish sin,
Prays all night long the wronged one may forgive,
  And suffer him and his in peace to live.

Notice how kindly all his prayer is heard,
  How speedily all that he asks is given,
How hate, that once his brother's heart so stirred,
  Is exorcised, and from him wholly driven,

THE VENTURE.

.And he goes joyfully, with hurrying feet
    The wanderer with forgiving kiss to greet.

See next a chosen people led away
    From bondage dire to a fair promised land,
Murmuring, rebelling, sinning, day by day,
    Till God in righteous anger lifts His hand
Saying, "Let me alone, let me alone,
    Till I my full destroying power have shown."

Mark with what earnestness the man who knows
    By years of trial the true worth of prayer,
Sends up the plea, "Nay, Lord, not upon those
    Heirs of thy covenant, thy tender care,
Wreak thy displeasure, wreak it upon me,
    At best a withered leaf, a fruitless tree."

Then note how quickly God is pacified,
    And with his cloudy pillar, all day long,
That glows like fire at night, deigns still to guide,
    Guard and sustain the stubborn, doubting throng,
Till journeying, danger, doubt and fear are o'er,
    And they rest safely on blest Canaan's shore.

Behold five heathen kings, with all their host
    Of warriors, eager to annihilate,
A few brave men, who, with no leader, post

THE VENTURE.   163

To meet them, heedless of the awful fate
Planned out for them, because their trust is staid
  On Him, whose counsel is, "Be not afraid."

See their brave leader bow his head in prayer,
  To God for help, for victory complete,
Then sure that he is heard and may declare,
  The joyful fact, the amazing words repeat,
"Sun, stand thou still, Moon, venture not to rise,
  Until this host, confused and vanquished, flies."

And lo! those mighty orbs, which ne'er before
  Had heeded any wish or word of man,
In meek obedience to the mandate, pour
  Motionless light upon the rear and van
Of that small army, till the day is done,
  Foes fled and glorious victory fairly won.

Next hear a childless wife her longings plead,
  Till God in pity listening to her prayer,
Sends her a son to be a wondrous seed,
  A priest, a judge, whom all men shall declare
A holy man, worthy the priestly name,
  Worthy forevermore of noble fame.

See there a king upon a sick-bed laid,
  Told by the prophets he must shortly die,

THE VENTURE.

Turn to the wall, regretful and dismayed,
　And pray for lengthened days, till the reply
Is sent, "Cease all thy moans and prayers and tears,
　Unto thy life is added fifteen years."

Look at that city, once so grandly great,
　Now desolated, and the faithful few
Inhabitants who share its changed estate,
　Despised, oppressed, not knowing what to do,
And lo! in answer to the prophet's prayer,
　All is transformed, changed to a picture fair.

Later, behold a chosen people doomed
　By the proud hate of a base mind to be
Wholly exterminated and entombed
　All in one day because one brave man's knee
· Bends not in cringing homage to a slave,
　An arrant coward and unpitying knave.

Then mark what prayer achieves when all is known
　To the fair queen, whose people and own life
Had been in jeopardy.　How though alone,
　Or few in number, in each time of strife,
For might and mastery, how God's people win,
　The victory, and reverse the plots of sin.

Then seek the furnace hot, the lions' den,
　Behold, the men of prayer walk brave and strong,

THE VENTURE. 165

Unscathed, untouched, endeavoring there and then
  To tell all doubters by triumphant song
God for his children has a constant care,
  Marks all their woes and hears their faintest prayer.

Next go to that grand palace, where a king
  Perplexed, astonished, sits in wild despair,
Because sly memory has refused to bring
  Before his mind the vision, foul or fair,
Which, while he slept, the dream-god's magic wand
  Caused in his presence for a while to stand.

See how, when all his efforts futile prove,
  He bids the wise men of his kingdom come,
And says in stern command, "E'en as ye love
  Your lives, sit not supinely grieved or dumb,
But show at once my vanished dream to me,
  And tell me truly what its import be."

Hear them cry out, indignant and astound,
  "O, King, tell us thy dream and we will show
The meaning or interpretation joined
  Thereto, but to make known the dream, you know
That never yet did potentate or king
  Demand so strange, impossible a thing."

THE VENTURE.

And while unmoved his order he repeats,
    And all the wise men tremble, wail and weep,
See Daniel and his friends seek their retreats
    And humbly pray their God long pledged to keep
Covenant and mercy, graciously to show
    The vision which had vexed their monarch so.

Notice how quickly their united pleas
    Prevail and win the curious favor sought,
And Daniel, wise to utter prophecies,
    Is to the troubled monarch's presence brought,
And tells him dream and meaning, till he cries,
    "Your God is Lord of gods, all true, all wise."

Consider, too, the many, many more
    Men of prophetic days, who in each hour
Of danger or of need, were wont to pour
    Into God's ear their pleas, until his power
Was manifested in the good they sought,
    And doubting souls to pray with faith were taught.

Think now of Olivet and that blest day
    When Jesus to the multitude declared
We are earth's blessed ones, and bade all pray—
    Not as the Pharisee, who proudly bared
His piety, saying time and again,
    "God, I thank thee, I'm not like other men."

THE VENTURE.

Bade them in humble, universal love,
  Rich, poor, high, low, kings, subjects, bond or
    free,
All pray, "Our Father, who in heaven above
  Art housed, and on earth should likewise be
OUR FATHER, by whose power we live,
  As Thou forgivest us, may we forgive."

Go to that mountain top whereon He knelt,
  While all within the valley lay asleep;
Think how His tender, loving spirit felt,
  What anguish wrung His heart, when he could
    weep
For those who dared His holiness deride,
  Dared shout, "Away! Let Him be crucified!"

Hear Him when lifting up His eyes to heaven
  After his final supper and address—
More eloquent than all he yet had given—
  Pray: "Father, keep and sanctify and bless
These, and all others whom Thou givest me,
  And make them all as one—as one in Thee."

Behold him in the garden struggling sore
  With nature and the innate love of life;
Hear how he utters o'er and o'er and o'er,
  "Not as I will," yet cannot end the strife

THE VENTURE.

'Twix will and nature, till the pitying day
  Bids the hard night of conflict pass away.

Then watch Him calmly go to meet His fate,
  Of crucifixion for humanity,
Heedless that many madly scoff and prate,
  Trying to prove that no divinity
Attaches to Him; praying as He goes,
  For blessings, ceaseless blessings on His foes.

Later, behold Him on the cruel cross,
  With bleeding hands and side, and thorn-crowned
    head,
Did ever man assume so great a loss?
  Was ever blood so pure, so precious, shed?
Did ever air resound a nobler cry?
  "Forgive them, it is finished, I can die."

Then hear the apostles as they go their way
  After their last commission, to proclaim
The Gospel tidings, hear them humbly pray
  For what they want, in their dear Master's name,
And learn from the emphatic answers given
  How prayer unlocks the treasure stores of Heaven.

Think, too, of the unnumbered faithful souls,
  Who since the world began have asked in prayer

THE VENTURE.

Of Him who all the universe controls,
  Whate'er they wished or needed, larger share
Of wisdom, grace or earth's material things,
  And lo! it come, borne by swift angel wings.

Think of all these, then humbly kneel and pray,
  Whenever you are tempted or dismayed,
Put doubt and fear far from your mind away,
  Have faith, and pray as you have never prayed,
So shall the ear, the eye, the heart, the hand,
  Of the Almighty God for you have care,
And you each day more fully understand
  The privilege, the power, the worth of prayer.

GOD'S PATIENCE AND GOD'S PEOPLE.

Malicious foes burning with jealous hate,
Spies, whisperers, and blasphemous perjurers,
May in concerted phalanx compass them,
Deprive them of all weapons, all defence,
Demolish every refuge they descry,
Increase their burdens, bind them hand and foot,
Put out their eyes and shut them into cells,
Shockingly foul, utterly desolate,
Dark as was chaos when the voice of God
Pierced it with that imperative command,

THE VENTURE.

"Let there be light;" yes, more, may silence them,
Scourge them and rack them most amazingly,
Threaten and menace them with torments new,
At morn, at noon and when the even-tide
Pronounces its blest benediction, "Rest;"
Relentlessly may carry on their work,
Ineffably and consumately base,
Till they have wrested from their victims all
But life, sheer life, and only sparing it
That they may add to their own infamy
As cruelty insatiate may suggest,
By mockery, insult, arrogance and show
Of triumph o'er their utter misery.

All this the enemies of those who trust
In God as long declared, Mighty to save,
Strong to deliver and to recompense,
Defiantly have done, are doing now,
While He, their pledged protector, father, friend,
In seeming heedlessness permits the wrong,
The base oppression, having reasons good,
Although they to our comprehension are
Wholly inscrutable, or worse than that,
Appear unjust.

Yet let no one who God's great patience dares,
And His forbearance mocks, hope to escape

THE VENTURE. 171

Unpunished for their rash presumptuousness,
For in His own good time He will draw near
Unto His trusting, tortured, wearied heirs,
In tenderest pity, and will comfort them,
Abundantly, while on their reckless foes
So very confident He would not heed
Or care for what they did or planned to do,
He will look down in righteous, angry scorn,
In furious indignation that will break
Their haughty power and wither it away
As grass is withered when the summer sun
Pours down his hottest rays in time of drought,
And while they cringe and cower in their surprise,
Stopping their fiendish work because they must,
And not because they are in some degree
Repentant for the suffering they have caused,
God, to His people more than doubly dear,
To Him for what they suffer, or unto
Their faithful friends who shared their lot of woe
In spirit, if not in the active sense,
He will give power, permission and command,
To wreak out vengeance, greater for delay,
Speedily on their enemies and His;
Give them the right, the honored privilege
Fully to prove His perfect righteousness;
To prove to all gainsaying, doubtless He

THE VENTURE.

Loves justice even as He loves Himself,
Not that it has intrinsic exellence
When unapplied, unexercised, unused,
But that it is in very great degree
One of His most exalted attributes,
With which He can not for one moment part,
Without large abdigation of what makes
His perfect total of majestic worth,
Glory and excellence, which ne'er can be
Equalled, much less excelled, tho' we should try
Throughout all time and all eternity,
Try constantly, with highest wrought up zeal,
Excelling in its force by vast degrees
All that we reckon zeal; that mercy which
Proves so conclusively His fatherhood,
His loving care, his tireless, watchful heed
Of each and everything that helps to make
The full, grand whole of the vast universe.

O, gloriously wonderful, among
God's many graces and high attributes,
Shines forth His perfect patience toward those
Who wrong His people and defy His power,
And comforting, exceeding comforting
Is the assurance of God's constant care
For all who humbly put their trust in Him

THE VENTURE. 173

While traveling the devious paths of earth,
Thronged as they are with many enemies,
Who ask no higher pleasure than to grieve,
Perplex, oppress and hinder all who say
They are but pilgrims seeking for a home,
A heavenly country, far from mortal ken,
Where they will nevermore through the dark glass
Of hope, anticipation or desire
Dimly behold the glories that surround
Him, whose almighty power and sovereign will
Decreed as part of His creative work
Their individual, actual entity
Decreed that they should sojourn for a while
As one among vast millions, who must learn
By weary wandering, the worth of rest;
By frequent strife, the priceless good of peace;
By doeful doubt and sad uncertainity,
The blessedness of all release therefrom;
By pain, how sweet exemption from pain is;
By loss, the exultant and abiding joy
Possession full and permanent create;
Learn by long dreading of that change called death,
The worth of life, of blest, immortal life;
Learn hourly, daily, o'er and o'er again,
The real, intrinsic worth of everything,
Lovely or precious or desirable,

174   *THE VENTURE.*

To make existence altogether blest,
And most supremely blest forevermore.

A STORY AND A SERMON.

"Be employed," remarked the parson,
    Then he bowed and went away,
Leaving me alone to wonder
    How he chanced the words to say,
For I was no idle dreamer,
    Well I knew it, so did he,
And I wondered much and questioned
    Why he spake those words to me.

I was sick, too sick for working,
    And my spirit was so sad
That the comforts round me lying
    Wholly failed to make me glad,
Life appeared a weary struggle,
    Costing more than it was worth,
And the hour of death seemed sweeter
    Than the moment of my birth.

But all this I had not told him,
    Our remarks were commonplace,
If he knew I was discouraged,

THE VENTURE.

It was only by my face.
So I wondered and I questioned
  Whether I should praise or blame
One who thus commended labor
  For a sick and wearied frame.

Yet, because I knew he seldom
  Spoke, except with kind intent,
And that though he uttered little,
  Very often much was meant.
I was certain that a sermon
  Or a lecture was annexed,
For my grave consideration
  To his briefly uttered text.

He had told a little story
  Of a man infirm and blind,
Who while languishing in prison,
  Fearing he might lose his mind,
Or in plainer, common parlance,
  Would "go crazy," now and then
Spent his time in quickly dropping
  Pins, to pick them up again.

I had laughed about the story,
  I had said, "The man was wise,
A philosopher, a genius,

THE VENTURE.

Worthy of applaud and prize."
But although our admiration
  Of an action may be great,
We may have no inclination
  Nor desire to imitate.

Dropping pins was not my fancy,
  And I was so very tired
That I felt to active labor
  I could not be forced nor hired,
So I said, " 'Tis surely giving
  Amiability a test
Thus to talk about employment
  To a person seeking rest."

Then I pressed upon the pillow
  Closer still my aching head,
But my mind kept on repeating
  What he had so briefly said.
And while thinking and while trying
  What might be implied, to find
Pleasant thoughts and good suggestions
  Flashed like sunbeams through my mind.

And my spirit rose in triumph,
  From its night of grief and pain,

THE VENTURE. 177

Saying, "Tho' too sick to labor,
  I will not exist in vain,
And the parson's brief injunction,
  "Be employed," shall be a text
From which I will make a sermon
  For the suffering and perplexed."

First, it is quite clear that pastime
  Should not be our only aim,
Long as every soul around us
  Has upon our care a claim,
And although we can not labor,
  We can speak in cheerful tones,
We can keep from endless murmurs,
  And unnecessary moans.

Secondly, 'tis always wiser
  To be hopeful, cheerful, kind,
Than to let our cares and troubles
  Rule like tyrants o'er the mind.
For tho' hard may be our pathway,
  And the work we have to do,
Still, *the bright side is the right side,*
  And *the kind way is the true.*

Thirdly, to us all are given
  Talents, either one or ten,

THE VENTURE.

And we all can do a little
  For our suffering fellow-men.
Tho' we can not rule the nation,
  We at least the laws can keep,
We can give a cup of water,
  Or can hush a child to sleep.

Fourthly, life is given for action,
  And the world is very wide,
Fields all white, all ripe for harvest,
  Wait us upon every side.
If we have a willing spirit,
  We can find enough to do,
And at last can show the Master
  Precious sheaves, not small nor few.

Fifthly, it is very certain
  That we never need despair,
Long as God from Heaven is watching
  O'er the world with Father care,
And while He to wild ambition
  Gives a check, or says, "Be still,"
We should rest without complaining,
  Meekly bowing to His will.

Finally, 'tis plain that *labor*,
  Which so many deem a *curse*,

THE VENTURE. 179

Brought on us by Eve and Adam,
    Is entirely the reverse,
And 'tis just as plain existence
    Will far better be enjoyed
If we make our daily motto,
    " Work for others, be employed."

WOMAN'S MISSION AND WOMAN'S WORK.

Her mission, to make homes and resting places
    Edens on earth,
Where men may rest from toil and prove her graces,
    Her precious worth.

Her mission, to see other lives out-growing
    From her frail frame;
Her work, to note all grief, all wayward-going,
    And shield from blame.

Her mission, to rebuke by virtuous life
    Vileness and sin;
Her work, to aid the erring in their strife
    Lost strength to win.

Her mission, to be strong and brave and wise,
    When man is weak;

THE VENTURE.

Her work, with love-light sparkling in her eyes,
　　Right words to speak.

Her mission, to be patient, faithful, true,
　　Though man be false;
Her work, to do all that God bids her do,
　　Though flesh revolts,

Her mission, that of a bright star, to lead
　　To Heaven and God;
Her work to soothe when man must smart and bleed
　　Beneath the rod.

Her mission, to speak words of hope and cheer
　　In man's sad hours;
Her work, to strew his path, when dark or drear,
　　With love's sweet flowers,

Her mission, in prosperity's bright day,
　　Praises to sing;
Her work, in adverse times, for grace to pray,
　　And aid to bring.

Her mission, in man's thoughtless, reckless hours,
　　To warn and grieve;
Her work, when pain and death reveal their powers,
　　To seek reprieve.

THE VENTURE.

Her mission, man's true helper every hour
 Of life to be,
His *guardian angel*, from the tempter's power,
 Leading him free.

Her mission, with true woman tact and skill,
 Life's journey through,
A thousand things which man nor can nor will,
 Daily to do.

Her mission, in a way heroic, wise,
 Sublime, divine,
To keep herself a constant sacrifice
 On duty's shrine.

Her work, to censure and reprove and chide,
 Condemn, command,
To teach, to lead, counsel, persuade, guard, guide,
 Nourish, defend.

Her work, to waken tenderness and love,
 And sweet-voiced hope,
And joy in other lives till joys above
 To her shall ope.

182 *THE VENTURE.*

THE MENAGERIE.

The fool may speak the wicked thought,
 "There is no God," but we who stand
Before these living trophies, brought
  From many a clime and many a land,
Dare not repeat the foolish words,
  For ceaselessly from all the throng
Of parti-colored beasts and birds,
  There comes a refutation strong.

The lion bold, the timid hare,
  The tiger fierce, the gentle dove,
Each in emphatic ways declare
  What wicked men would fain disprove:
Each joins to say there is a power
  Controlling nature everywhere,
And guarding every day and hour
  Each living thing with tender care.

And *man*, at once creation's crown,
  Its lord and master, proudly stands,
Or meekly, calmly sitting down,
  Lifts up to Heaven his powerful hands,
And echoes in triumphant tones
  The wise assertion of a God,

THE VENTURE. · 183

Who counts the stars, makes seas and zones,
  Bestows the crown or wields the rod.

And *woman*, yet more large or small,
  Than nature meant that she should be,
Her homeward hurrying sisters call,
  And bids them pause awhile and see
How nature can reverse her laws,
  Compress, or at her will expand,
And preach a God, a great First Cause,
  In every age and every land.

WONDERINGS.

  A century from now
Where and what will we be?
  A century from now
What changes shall we see?
  Will Time move on the same
Exact, invarying round?
  Men question whence they came,
And whither they are bound?

  A century from now
Whose lips will speak our name?
  Whose heart exult that we
To earth as dwellers came?

184 · *THE VENTURE.*

If dead, who seek our tomb
To drop affection's tear,
 Or sit in grief and gloom
Because we are not here?

 A century from now
We will be greatly changed,
 On each surviving brow
Deep furrows will be ranged.
 Time will move on the same,
The sun will rise and set,
 And others praise and blame,
Remember and forget.

CITY TREES

I love them, I love them, the trees of the city,
Which beautify by-streets, and dot even marts,
 Seeming imbued with a generous pity
For the people who labor with nature-starved hearts,
 Who wearily long for the cool, shady forests,
The orchards, the gardens, where gay hours were spent,
 For the fields and the meadows, the glades and the
 wildwoods,
Which they roamed and explored with delighted con-
 tent.

THE VENTURE.

I love them, I love them, the trees of the city,
In spring-time and summer and autumn's ripe hours,
  In winter, when no trace of verdure remaineth,
To show the effects of warm sunbeams and showers.
  To tell of a God who loves all he createth,
Who keeps in His storehouse of merciful care,
  For each proof of his skill and beneficent wisdom
Sustenance ample, enough and to spare.

I love them, I love them, the trees of the city,
  That soften the hard lines of science and art;
That shade with an angel-like patience and pity
  The toil-worn, the tempted, the broken in heart;
That speak to the old of the past and its lessons,
  That sing to the young of the truths they must learn,
That say to each being who hears or beholds them
  "Of dust thou art made and to dust must return."

Right dearly I love them, and think a rich blessing
Is due those who plant them, in beauty to thrive,
  To make for the song-birds safe places for nesting
Orchestras wherefrom they may often revive
  In our minds, faith in God as our Maker, our Father,
Trust in Him as our guide and unchangeable friend,
  Who, tho' he may lead us through trial and trouble,
In peace will at last bid our wanderings end.

THE VENTURE.

LABOR AND CAPITAL.

Said Labor to Capital, "You have money,
   Money that wonderful things can do,
While I have muscles, brain and muscles,
   In measure to profit both me and you.

"If you care to pay a certain stipend,
   A lawful price for a given while,
I will labor for you. Is it a bargain?
   Shall I take for 'yes' your quiet smile?"

Capital answered, proudly, coldly,
   In tones of a master, not a friend:
"If to employ you, try your labor,
   I for a season do condescend,

"Know and remember, each hour remember,
   Your strength and time are mine, all mine,
From the earliest dawn of every morning,
   Till the orbs of evening begin to shine."

"But you forget, forget," said Labor,
   "I am human as well as you,
Requiring rest and recreation
   To make and keep me to nature true."

THE VENTURE.

Capital sneered, "To me that's nothing,
  All that I want is your faithful toil,
You are a fighter with fate, my business
  Is the adding of golden spoil to spoil."

As plead fond parents with their children
  Who err; as pleadeth man and wife,
As plead the oppressed for right and justice,
  As plead the doomed to die, for life,

So Labor pleaded for the people,
  The fragile women, stalwart men,
God's honorable, toil-burdened children,
  Who briefly rest, then toil again.

But Capital proudly scorned all pleadings,
  Till growing desperate, Labor cried:
"You may laugh and sneer, but the fact is patent,
  Eight hours is a figure on your side.

"Yes, a figure, sir, I might say fortune,
  For o'er worked muscles can never do
Work that will equal the work accomplished
  By workers whose laboring hours are few.

"Search the world through, and those who labor
  Without cessation, for thirteen hours,

188 *THE VENTURE.*

Tremble and falter, and over and over
  Stamp in their work 'exhausted powers.'

"While those who toil for a shorter season,
  Prove by their zest and efficient skill
That they who demand the longest labor
  For the poorest work pay the heaviest bill."

"Humph," said Capital, "You are a striker,
  And that last stroke, sir, is pretty strong,
I'll think about it, and time will settle
  Whether your views or mine are wrong."

NATAL BELLS.

Our natal bells, how oft they tell
How rapidly the seasons roll,
How swiftly grows our being's scroll.

The helpless babe is soon the child,
The sanguine youth, with fancies wild,
The adult, more moderate, calm and mild.

Rashly, or with a cautious art,
With honest or deceitful heart,
We act in Life's long play our part.

THE VENTURE.

Tho' both our creed and course be wrong,
Heedless alike of sigh or song,
Time moves us rapidly along.

Past many a verdant isle, where we
Fancy to dwell would surely be
Completeness of felicity.

Past icebergs of sore loss and grief,
Past many a troublous rock and reef,
He speeds us like a floating leaf.

Or like a foam-capped ocean-wave,
Designed some far-off shore to lave,
Rolls us from cradle-bed to grave.

And fears and hopes by turns prevail,
While eyes grow dim and cheeks grow pale,
And steps more slow, and spirits fail.

Yet how we live, and how we grow,
And how our lives in currents flow,
We for ourselves alone can know.

For life and growth, tho' common things,
As free to subjects as to kings,
Move evermore with noiseless wings.

THE VENTURE.

And all we of their mystery know,
Is that we are, and that we grow,
And must forever onward go.

And while we strive for bread and gold,
Our natal bells are promptly tolled,
And we are classed among the old.

Thus onward seasons swiftly roll,
Longer our birth-bells yearly toll,
And larger grows life's mystic scroll.

Until a time no human ken
Unerringly can name, and then,
We change, and from the haunts of men

Depart to spiritual spheres,
To learn through all succeeding years
The "why" of earthly toils and tears.

Our natal bells are like a voice
Speaking in words of wisdom choice,
Bidding us all in life rejoice.

Bidding us everywhere we go
Mitigate others' weight of woe,
And seeds of kindness freely sow.

THE VENTURE. 191

Fully assured that Time will bring
For each good deed some precious thing
To swell Right's final harvesting.

A BIT OF BLANK VERSE.

As earth is made of atoms, so this thing
This essence, this warm state which we call life,
Is made of little things, short breaths and sighs,
Short steps, brief glances, smiles and tears and
Succeeding one another measuredly,   [words,
Quick heart-throbs and slow pulse-beats, proving
Is strong or feeble, as the red blood flows   [force
With even or uneven measurings.

The form is not the measure of the being,
Earth's circuit round.   It is the mind, the heart,
The soul, the immortal soul, that ever makes
The full, ripe nature; form, itself, may be
Of Liliputian mold, or grown so gross
As to offend all those who love to gaze
On symmetry and beauty, yet the soul
Enshrined therein, may be as large, or fair
Or grandly perfect as e'er glorified
A human frame of the most faultless mould.

THE VENTURE.

Pow'rs may be fettered, cramped or crippled sore,
Yet be quite perfect in their innate strength,
Their natural scope and capability
And all degrees or points essential to
Efficient labor and the winning of
Unstinted approbation and reward.
Or we, perchance, may be compelled to dwell
In lonely, uncongenial social folds,
In dreary nooks and corners all the while
Our aspiration reaches highest Heaven,
And our ambition compasses the world.

We are not now what we were yesterday,
We do not think like thoughts or speak like words,
Nor are we what we will be, every hour.
We change, we grow, and, if we will it, may
Grow better, upward, outward, every day,
Until we sleep, to wake from Time's short night
To an eternal day of blessedness,
Whence looking back across the gulf of space,
Which separates this world from the Above,
Life, which we now consider wonderful,
Will seem more wonderful, more precious still,
And we shall know ourselves and see how small,
How impotent we are, beside that God   [Cause,
Who rules supreme, earth's glorious Great First

THE VENTURE. 193

Lord of the Universe, First King of Heaven,
And our Creator, blessed evermore.

THE COPY.

" Better to live well than to live long,"
  The school-boy wrote the copy o'er and o'er,
With graceful flourishes and careless scrawls,
  He wrote as many a boy had done before,
And when his sheet was full he laid it by,
  Thinking, "Again that copy I will try."

'Tis said, "The days of prophecy are past,"
  And they may be, but often as I look
Upon the page his pen had marked so fast,
  And read those words which so his fancy took,
I doubt the statement, and it seems to me
  That school-boy wrote his own life's prophecy.

For scarcely had he thought, "Those words are true,
  I'll heed their lesson, and my life shall be
Well spent, so well my teacher will not rue
  The hour he wrote this copy down for me,"
Ere the Death Angel touched him, and he lay
  With folded hands, cold as a lump of clay.

And I, who own that blotted paper now,
  And stand a weeper at his early grave,

THE VENTURE.

Repeat his copy, and remember how
　With generous, lavish way he daily gave
Friendship and love and trust to all who came
　Anear him holdîng out a hand or claim.

And while I look and weep and ponder well,
　I feel as tho' an angel spoke to me,
Bidding me tarry not, but haste to tell
　All that upon the blotted page I see,
Say to the young in story and in song:
　"'*Tis better to live well than to live long.*"

O, youth, so hopeful and so brave of heart!
　To whom this life seems all, yes, all you need,
O, maiden! whose pure lips so often part
　With merry laughter, giving little heed
To future years, but fancying it were well
　Here in this old queer world alway to dwell,

Pause, listen, for this life is not the whole
　Of our existence, tho' our joy be great
In its possession, evermore the soul,
　Our nobler part, sighs for a higher state,
Or realm, or sphere, where free from every woe
　It can perpetually expand and grow.

All this I read upon the scribbled page,
　And at the angel's bidding tell to you,

THE VENTURE. 195

For I have pledged my every power to wage
 War against sin, and for the good and true
To plead and toil, but if my words you scout,
 And proudly ask for more to clear your doubt,

Go ask all those who sold their hopes of Heaven
 For short-lived pleasure or a little gold,
If it has paid, and to you will be given
 When they speak true, in accents firm and bold,
" Nay, it has not, we did a mighty wrong,
" *'Tis better to live well than to live long.*"

And from the souls writhing in full despair,
 And from the spirits blest forevermore,
From all the evil and the good, like prayer
 Repeated daily, hourly, o'er and o'er,
Sounds on the air in accents clear and strong:
 " *'Tis better to live well than to live long.*"

THE ONE NAME.

There is one name that I would trace
 In richest gold and rarest gems,
Round which in forms of truest grace
 Would wreathe earth's grandest diadems;
One name, to which in humble awe
 And grateful homage I would bow,

THE VENTURE.

Offering as due sacrifice,
   Adoring love's most solemn vow;
One name, to which my soul would raise
   The incense of perpetual praise.

There is one name that I would speak
   With reverential, tender tone;
One name that I would ever seek,
   In all its richness to make known;
One name to which I long to see
   Earth's every dweller reverent kneel;
One name, whose praise I fain would hear
   Rise in one full, triumphant peal;
One name, than all sweet names more sweet,
   Whose praises angels oft repeat.

That name is Jesus! Hear, my soul,
   With reverent awe, that sacred name,
To make thee of life's sickness whole,
   Jesus to earth once kindly came;
For thee He lived a suffering life,
   Of hatred, scorn, neglect and blame;
For thee He bore the tempter's strife,
   For thee the keenest pain and shame;
For thee, for all, the Saviour died,
   The Son of God was crucified.

THE VENTURE.

Blest name, the pledge of love untold,
  Of pardon, peace and purity,
The only title we can hold
  Or plead as soul security,
Rest for the weary, joy for those
  With grief or weariness oppressed,
Hope's anchor, haven of repose,
  Through it life's ills are all redressed,
Through it our needs are all supplied,
  And God is fully satisfied.

Jesus! let those who dare deride,
  Let those who will, scoff and reject,
My soul in Thee will still confide,
  Shall still believe Thou wilt protect,
Still wilt I call thee Son of God,
  Redeemer, Intercessor, Friend,
Still seek for pardon through Thy blood,
  My hope's beginning and its end,
And if I perish, it shall be
  Trusting, Lord, Jesus Christ, in Thee.

198   *THE VENTURE.*

A PROTEST.

After reading the remark: "It is reported that —— is dead."

Say not that he is dead, the man who dared
  Bravely to speak the stern, indignant word
When, drunk with malice, jealous foes declared
  Evil of one whom he had ever heard
Kindly commended as a faithful friend
  Of the afflicted, the oppressed, the weak,
Of all who have an interest to defend
  A wrong to right, a privilege to seek.

Say not that he is dead, for such as he
  Are born immortal, and can never know
What death, real death is, they awhile may be
  In that cold, quiet state, which here below
Heaven and its life of perfect blessedness,
  We to designate from all other states
To which our human parts are more or less
  Subject, call *death*, the key to spirit gates.

But that is all, his spirit ne'er can die,
  It will but drop its tenement of clay,
Its perishable rind, and unseen fly
  As flies the air, away, away, away,
Upward and higher, till at length it gains

THE VENTURE. 199

Heaven and the presence of its maker, God,
There to be free from all that tempts or pains
Man, or brings on him the chastening rod.

FRIENDSHIP.

When hopes fondly cherished are blighted or flown,
And we among strangers are toiling alone,
Oft thinking with sorrow or yearning regret
Of old times, of past scenes, or of people we met,
Loved, trusted, and think till creation shall end
Will prove themselves worthy the sacred name, friend;
Or of others who taught us the lesson anew—
The fickle are legion, the steadfast are few,
Be the time dawn or mid-day or twilight's blest hour
When thus we are swayed by thought's magical power,
When thus we review, retrospect and look o'er,
Scenes, faces and forms we shall never see more,
How cheering the message from one who is true,
"You are not forgotten; we oft think of you."

"You are not forgotten," there's manna and balm,
Wine, oil, fragrant incense, gay song and grave psalm
In this precious assurance, this proof that old friends
Are faithful, whatever occurs or portends,
And thinking it over, the tried heart grows strong

THE VENTURE.

To bear the neglect of the merciless throng,
Grows strong to endure, struggle, strive and prevail,
Until duty is done, or until powers wholly fail,
Oh, Friendship, true Friendship! Time's bruises and
stings
Lose much of their poignance wherever thy wings
Are spread, or thou standest, a sheltering rock
To break the rough force of adversity's shock,
As long as the ages are circling round
Thy praise will be sung with joy high and profound.

·THE VALUE OF A SOUL.

Friend, wouldst thou know the value of a soul?
Go, count the stars, and give their number true;
Weigh the whole world, then write its perfect weight;
Value earth's every treasure at its worth,
Then add together number, weight and sum
And multiply their product by itself,
Time and again, until their figures reach
High as man's highest power can compute,
Then lay the whole within some balance true,
And in another I will lay a soul,
One single heaven-born soul, and you shall see
That as a mountain towers above a vale,
As grains of dust appear by tons of gold,

THE VENTURE. 201

So doth a single soul excel in worth
All things this side of Heaven.

A PROOF OF IMMORTALITY.

Suggested by reading the Grecian tradition of Ion and Clemantha.

"Shall we meet again, Clemantha?
　You this question ask of me,
And I of myself oft ask it,
　With intensest agony,
For tho' sweet thus for my country
　A sacrifice to be,
It is hard, Oh, hard, Clemantha,
　Thus to go away from thee.

"Shall we meet again, Clemantha?
　I have asked it of the hills,
I have asked it of the valleys,
　Through which flow the gleesome rills;
Of the trees, and of each insect
　That with life doth throb and hum,
Of the stars that shine in Heaven,
　But they all alike were dumb.

"Shall we meet again, Clemantha?
　When I look into thy face,

THE VENTURE.

When I note thy loving features
　Stamped with beauty and with grace,
When I see the love-light flashing
　From thine eyes so brightly plain,
Then I feel we are immortal,
　And that we shall meet again.

We shall meet again, Clemantha,
　And our greeting shall be sweet,
For no fear of separation
　Shall oppress us when we meet,
But our souls in sweet communion
　Shall forever joy and grow,
And our bliss be all the greater
　For our parting here below.

FINISHED WORK.

We look at things completed, and comment
Say perfect or defective, good or bad,
But think not of the long protracted toil,
The midnight vigils and the noontide sweats,
The circumstances totally adverse,
The trials, failures and discouragements,
The hours, the days, the aggregated weeks,
The months, perchance the years that were required

THE VENTURE. 203

To make it the perfected whole we see;
Ignore the strong, enthusiastic zeal
The noble, heaven-born, dauntless energy
Which made mistakes their helpers and secured
From each provoking failure some success,
Nor once relinquished hope, but went on bravely,
Wresting some victory from each delay
Of plan or purpose, this stupendous price
The worker or producer had to pay,
As license fee or legal premium,
Upon the work ere it could be completed,
We with injustice consumately utter
Omit as weightless, disconnected nothings,
Or waive as insignificant belongings,
And poising hastily the scales of judgment,
Our own weak, narrow judgment, place therein
The finished work, and with immense complacence
Our verdict give, sometimes of commendation,
And hasty praise, but often, full as often,
Of criticism, pitilessly cruel,
Or at the best uncharitably severe.

A SOLILOQUY.

No sound, no sound! no loudly chiming bell,
Nor cannon's boom nor wind's intensest roar,

THE VENTURE.

Nor thunder peal, nor ocean's loudest swell,
 Nor music, such as high-toned organs pour,
Or best strung harps yield from their secret store.

No sound, no sound! I dwell' alone, alone,
 In silence, such as reigns in deepest grave,
Not even my own voice in sigh or moan
 Starting a single ripple or sound wave
To flow until the shores of sense they lave.

No sound, no sound! Lost, wholly, wholly lost,
 Within myself to all by which the ear
Can to the mind reveal at trifling cost
 Causes for hope and joy or doubt and fear,
Or warning give that danger hovers near.

No sound, no sound! Silence on every side,
 A silence so profound no words can show
Its solemn perfectness, how like a tide
 Of cold, dead waters, without ebb or flow
It holds, engulfs and wears by tortures slow.

No sound, no sound! An alien, though at home,
 An exile, even in my native land,
A prisoner, too, for though at will I roam,
 Yet chained and manacled I oft must stand.
Unmoved, though sounds vibrate on every hand.

THE VENTURE. 205

No sound, no sound!   Yet often I have heard
  Echoing through dear memory's sacred hall
The buzz of bees, the rare song of a bird,
  The melody of raindrops as they fall,
The wind's wild notes or Sabbath bell's sweet call.

And often, too, in memory I hear
  My parents telling me, in songs, of Heaven,
That happy land, that wholly blissful sphere
  Where hearts are ne'er by sin or trouble riven,
But all are blest, forgiving and forgiven.

No outward sound!   Yet often I perceive
  Kind angel voices speaking to my soul
Sweetly consoling changes to believe
  That this life is a part, and not the whole
Of being, its beginning, not its goal.

They tell me, too, a day is drawing near
  When all life's burdens I may lay aside,
And pass from earth into that blissful sphere
  Lying beyond the intervening tide
Which we call death, and think so deep and wide.

No sound except the echoes of the past,
  Seeming at times, in tones now loud now low,
The voices of a congregation vast,

THE VENTURE.

Praising the God from whom all blessings flow,
Until my heart with rapture is aglow.

No pleasant sound, yet I am well content
  To wait until the Master deigns to say
In tones by sympathy made eloquent,
  "It is enough, lo! thy deliverance day
Is dawning, weary prisoner, come away.

"Come, thou, who of my Father, God, art blessed,
  Inherit now the kingdom that for you
He hath prepared, the satisfying rest,
  The peace that passeth not like morning dew,
The joy perpetual yet forever new."

Sweet words, if they shall be the first to break
  The silence of these swiftly-fleeting years,
What a grand recompense!   Henceforth I make
  Them the assuagers of my sighs and tears,
The kind rebukers of my doubts and fears.

WHAT I WOULD DO.

I long to strike the poet's harp
  ·Till it sends forth such melody
That every ear on which it falls
  Shall thrill with wondering ecstacy.

THE VENTURE.

Oh, I would waken notes sublime,
　To cheer the hearts now sad with grief,
And lull them for a blissful time
　Into a sense of sweet relief.

And I would sing again the songs
　The angels sing on heavenly hills,
Which echo down to me prolongs
　Until my soul with rapture thrills,
Sing them in notes so rarely sweet
　That they would charm each toil-dulled ear,
And woo the pleasure-seeking crowd
　To pause awhile and wondering hear.

And I would clothe in words the thoughts
　The glorious thoughts that come to me,
Fresh from Truth's mine, golden ingots,
　Gems of rare hue and purity,
Oh, I would write them down in words
　Noted for strength and eloquence,
And send them broadcast o'er the world
　Accomplishing Heaven's wise intents.

But I am weak, I can not strike
　The poet's harp with skillful hand,
I can not wake rare melodies
　To be re-echoed through the land;

THE VENTURE.

Too puny is my strength to clothe
   With master power the precious thoughts
That come and pass from out my mind,
   Glittering like gems and rich ingots.

What then? Shall I ignobly wait
   As those who gaze at vacancy,
Or murmur that my talents rate
   Only plain mediocrity?
No, I will take the poet's harp
   And strike at least its simple keys,
Trusting that in some stronger soul
   They may rouse higher melodies.

And as my strength, my skill permits,
   I'll clothe the thoughts that come to me,
And send them out, mere waifs and bits
   To float o'er human life's great sea,
Praying that they may prove to some
   Discouraged, grief-tossed voyager
A friendly spar to save it from
   The yawning whirlpool of despair.

And having toiled with head and hand,
   I will await with conscience clear
Till I before the Judge must stand
   His verdict on my toil to hear,

THE VENTURE.

Wait past all doubting, firmly sure
That justice will not make it naught,
Because that I, with motives pure
According to my strength have wrought.

WHEN I SHALL BE SATISFIED.

Though now I see no purpose in my life,
Nor understand the mystery of its plan,
Nor know how far beyond the present hour
      Extends its sphere,
If when the span is measured, it appears
That God through my poor life was glorified,
Though now I see nothing but mystery,
      I shall be satisfied.

Though now I bear pain's heavy, galling cross,
And sorrow wounds my heart to bitter tears,
And all the gold of joy is mixed with dross,
      If it appears
When all is ended, that my heavy cross
Was but my crown, bent thus, its worth to hide,
And every trial was a well-set gem,
      I shall be satisfied.

Though toil has brought me small material gain,
And every year is marked with heavy loss,

210   *THE VENTURE.*

And tho' my graves of disappointed hopes
    Are green with moss,
If, when the Master comes to view my work,
And lay it in His balance to be tried,
I find that others were enriched thereby,
    I shall be satisfied.

Tho' now my heart gives more than it receives,
And much that others value is denied
To me, from day to day, if Death reveals
    What life doth hide,
And proves beyond all doubting that each wish
Each want of mind and heart here unsupplied
Purchased some pleasure for another life,
    I shall be satisfied.

BRING FLOWERS.

" They speak of hope to the fainting heart,
With a bud of promise they come and part,
  They sleep in dust through the wintry hours,
They break forth in glory—bring flowers, bright flowers."
      —Mrs Hemans.

Bring flowers, fresh flowers, when the joyful sing,
  At the birth and the solemn christening,
They are emblems true of our mortal state,
  Of its end, its certain, avoidless fate,

THE VENTURE.

Like them awhile shall the infant grow,
  Like them at last in the dust lay low,
Then fail not, oh, fail not fresh flowers to bring
  For the natal day and the christening.

Bring flowers for the bridal when hope tow'rs high,
  And love is beaming from lip and eye,
When fear and doubt and distrust are still,
  And joy is toning each pulse's thrill,
When trust is with perfect trust repaid,
  And a solemn, mutual compact made,
And life is sweet, Oh, then bring flowers,
  To bless with their beauty the fleeting hours.

Bring flowers to speak of the love Divine,
  That measures love's farthest boundary line,
That notes the fitness of each for each,
  And hears the thought tho' unformed in speech,
Bring flowers to tell us that tho' decay
  Our strength and vigor may steal away,
The love that is true shall never die,
  But will add to the bliss of our home on high.

Bring flowers for the coffin o'er which we weep
  For the friend whom we vainly strove to keep
From the spoiler's hand and his chilling breath

THE VENTURE.

When he came to work that change called death,
To transplant the soul to us so dear
　To a richer soil and a higher sphere,
Bring flowers, they will speak of the spirit's bloom
　While the flesh decays in the silent tomb.

Bring flowers, sweet flowers, when the trusting
　　heart
　With its darling joys is forced to part,
When its budding hopes all droop and die,
　And its idols in broken fragments lie,
When faith is wavering, courage fled,
　And doubt's dark pall over life is spread,
Oh, then bring flowers, sweet flowers, to prove
　Almighty power and unfailing love.

Bring flowers at morn, at noon, at night,
　To cheer our souls while they charm our sight,
To rebuke our murmurs and hush our fears,
　With their whispers of past and of coming years.
Bring flowers to tell us that grief shall cease,
　And toil be crowned with a due increase,
In all life's stages and fleeting hours,
　Bring flowers, bring beautiful, fragrant flowers.

THE VENTURE. 213

A LITTLE WHILE.

A little while to walk life's rugged road,
  A little while to bear its heavy load,
A little while to labor and to weep,
  A little while earth's scattered grains to reap.

A little while, and then, life's toils all o'er,
  Its trials past, its sorrows felt no more,
The soul safe in its many-mansioned home,
  Shall be at rest, thence nevermore to roam.

A little while, help us, dear Father, God,
  To bear with patience every cross and load,
Help us with faith to labor on to Thee,
  And meekly wait until Thou set'st us free.

Free to behold Thee in Thy glorious home,
  Free from Thy presence nevermore to roam,
Free to adore Thee, to bask in Thy smile,
  Free evermore, not for a little while.

GOOD AND BETTER.

  To die, O, it were sweet!
To bid adieu to sorrow, loss and care,
  To fold the weary hands, compose the feet,

THE VENTURE.

And nevermore to breathe an anxious prayer;
  To say a few faint words of kind "good-night,"
To the few friends whom we consider true,
  Then close the eyes to earth's poor, fitful light,
And open them on scenes sublimely new.

    To live, O, it is grand!
When disappointment, trouble, loss and pain
  Have tracked us on and on, until we stand
Convinced that unsubstantial, poor and vain
  Are the right names for much we mortals seek
And struggle for most pertinaciously,
  Till God draws near, rebuking words to speak,
And take our idols one by one away.

    To live, O, it is sweet!
Each day, each hour, we live to strive to be
  A blessing to each soul we chance to meet
Lovingly helping it to feel and see
  Life is worth living, is a precious boon,
A wholly precious boon, although the heart
  Before we have attained our prime, our noon,
Has with its dearest hopes been forced to part.

    To live, O, it is grand!
To live not for one's self and friends alone,
  But for each troubled soul whose trembling hand

THE VENTURE.

Is raised to Heaven, whose agonizing moan
  Echoes through space, onward from sphere to
      sphere,
Onward through each celestial clime and zone,
  Until it reaches the all-pitying ear
Of Him who sits on Heaven's eternal throne.

    · To live, O, it is sweet!
Self-will, self-love, self-righteousness and sin
  Of every kind, to trample neath our feet,
And daily sanguine victories to win,
  In heart, in mind, in body and in soul,
O'er eye and ear, o'er tongue and lip and hand,
  O'er all that makes our individual whole,
O, thus to live is truly sweet and grand.

LINES FOR A YOUNG LADY'S ALBUM.

    A moment is a little thing,
      Made up of seconds small,
    An hour, what is it? A short string
      Of moments—that is all.

    Days are but aggregated hours,
      Weeks, only days combined;
    Months are but weeks of sun and shower,
      Named, numbered and defined.

216   *THE VENTURE.*

Days, weeks, months, years, which come
          and go
    With ceaseless, noiseless speed,
Leaving us pleasure, pain or woe,
    Plenty, or pinching need,

Into vast ages, by the tide
    Of time, with speed of thought,
Are added, weighed or multiplied,
    And from them all are wrought

Eternity, that circle great,
    Older than human ken;
Life-time of God and seal of fate,
    To angels and to men.

Determine then, Time's fragments small
    So wisely to employ,
Eternity for one and all
    Will bear a stamp of joy.

COUNSEL FOR THE TROUBLED.

What though friends to-day forsake thee,
    Love them still;
From thy valley kindly watch them
    Climb life's hill.

THE VENTURE. 217

What though pain may torture keenly,
    Patient be,
Keenest pain is soonest over,
    Thou wilt see.

What though sorrow be thy birthright,
    Smile and sing,
Roses have their thorns and honey
    Has its sting.

What though disappointment track thee,
    Never mind,
Read we upon all life's changes
    God is kind.

Read we too, the blest assurance
    "Fleeting fast,
Pain and grief and all life's trials
    Soon are past."

LIFE IS LIKE THE WEATHER.

Life, sweet friend, is like the weather,
    Rough and pleasant, warm and cold,
Bright and dark with variations,
    Wonderful and manifold.

THE VENTURE.

Every heart must have its winter,
　Every mind its autumn hours,
That more rich may be its harvests,
　And more gay its time of flowers.

As when clouds have spent their fullness,
　Nature looks more calmly sweet,
So our storms of pain and trouble
　Leave us more in faith complete.

Heaven's attractions would be lessened
　Had we less of trouble here,
We with earth would be contented,
　Wishing for no higher sphere.

And full many a heart now beating
　With a sympathetic thrill
For the griefs and pains of others,
　Would beat cold and selfish still.

Learn then thoroughly the lesson,
　Precious as the finest gold,
Which the changing skies and seasons
　So perpetually unfold.

Learn that all the days of trial
　We are wont to call adverse,

THE VENTURE. 219

Oftener far than we will credit,
  Are entirely the reverse.

Bear then patiently each sorrow,
  Pain or trouble, care or loss,
Which our Father adds or mingles
  To your cup or to your cross. .

And as surely as the winter
  Is succeeded by the spring,
Or the genial warmth of summer
  Genial autumn harvests bring,

Up, in bountiful perfection,
  In your heart will quickly grow
Tender sympathy for others
  In their times of bitter woe,

Giving that in liberal measure
  To each needy one you meet,
You will find, whate'er your station,
  Life is pleasant, even sweet.

Heed, therefore, each truth, each lesson
  Taught us by the changing skies,
And in every dismal prospect
  See some blessing in disguise.

NO ADVERSE CHANGE BEYOND THE TOMB.

The moss grows o'er the brick,
  The rust conceals the wire,
And time and change conflict
  With purpose and desire;
Trouble pursues our steps,
  And pain afflicts us sore,
And the bright star of youth
  Sets low, to rise no more.

But tho' the moss and rust
  Grow fast and gather thick,
And time and cruel change
  With our desires conflict,
The soul, beyond the tomb,
  Shall live when Time is o'er,
Most gloriously to bloom,
  Vernal forevermore.

For trouble, loss and grief
  Belong alone to earth,
They can not reach us when
  We pass our spirit's birth;
And every hope that fades

THE VENTURE.

And every joy that dies
Will help to make more blest
Our home beyond the skies.

TRUE REST.

Rest is not turning
From sorrow or care,
Selfishly spurning
All burdens to bear.

Rest is not waiting
For fortune to smile,
Gloomily prating
Of trouble the while.

Rest is not sitting
With hands idly clasped,
Watching time flitting
Away to the past.

'Tis earnestly aiming
Each duty to do,
For failures ne'er framing
Excuses untrue.

'Tis meekly receiving
What God deemeth best,

THE VENTURE.

Obeying, believing,
This, this *is true rest.*

THANKSGIVING LINES.

For life, wonderful mystery
That animates and moves our frames,
That makes us objects of Thy love,
And presses on that love large claims,
We thank Thee, O, Thou source of life,
For the rich boon thy hand has given,
For mortal life, in which to grow
Meet for the higher life of Heaven.

For light, that mystery great as life,
That confluence of etheral streams,
That flows around us, day and night,
Through sun or moon or stars mild beams,
We offer thanks and praise to Thee,
Thou great primeval source of light,
Whose bright effulgence shall outshine
All glories which now greet our sight.

For friends, those who in weal or woe
Love, trust us, and believe us true,
Who bid us hope when grief is sent
Our hearts to chasten and subdue.

THE VENTURE.

To Thee, man's first and truest friend,
We offer now our thanks, and pray
   Thou wilt, where'er our steps may tend,
Still be our friend and guide alway.

For every joy that makes life sweet,
Or hope that mitigates our woe,
   For all the varied good which Thou
Hast deigned upon us to bestow,
   We thank Thee, Father, just and wise,
And while we thank Thee, humbly pray,
   Grant us Thy mercy, love and care
Long as we tread life's changeful way.

THE BIBLE.

Thou wouldst be wise, wisdom in it is found,
   Wisdom that will endure eternally,
Thou wouldst have wealth, treasures therein abound,
   Treasures that will enrich supernally.

Thou seekest purity, here is large store,
   Keep God's commands and purity is thine,
Beyond this he requires of us no more,
   Love and obedience are His boundary line.

Thou longest oftentimes for peace and rest.
   It tells of peace passing all human thought,

224   *THE VENTURE.*

Of rest in its vast perfectness so blest
   It with the blood of God's dear Son was bought.

And if for friendship thou dost sadly sigh
   It teaches of a friend ready to be
Close, close unto thy soul forever nigh,
   And truer than thy truest self to thee.

Here too, is comfort for the night of grief,
   And counsel for the days of joy and pride,
Chiding for the dark hours of unbelief,
   When hopes too fondly nursed have drooped and
      died.

Wisdom and wealth and purity and peace,
   Rest, friendship, counsel, all thy soul requires,
Worth to enhance or blessedness increase,
   Is here contained, despite both floods and fires.

WHERE IS CLIFFIE?

"Where is Cliffie?   Where is Cliffie?"
   Many, many times a day
  In a maze of anxious wonder,
   Questions lonely little May.
"I have called him, I have sought him,
   But my call and search were vain,

THE VENTURE.

Papa, Mamma, tell, Oh, tell me
　When will Cliffie come again?

"Where is Cliffie?　Aunty tell me,
　Why did he not come with you?
Has he lost his cap or mittens?
　Lost his ball or trumpet new?
Would not uncle help him find it,
　Or has he forgot the way
That he does not heed my calling,
　Does not come with me to play?

"Every day we played together,
　And were happy as each bird
That in spring or summer weather
　Makes its grateful gladness heard,
In sweet warblings, soft and tender,
　Gay, exultant, shrill and clear,
Heard till with delight and wonder
　Thrills each listening human ear."

Pityingly we note her questions,
　Kindly tell her not to cry,
Gently wipe each pearl-like tear-drop
　From each soulful little eye,
But the while our hearts are bleeding,
　And our tears are falling fast,

THE VENTURE.

And we ask why buds of promise
  Prematurely droop and blast.

Ask with anxious, grieving wonder
  Why so much of loss and woe
Is the portion of God's people
  While they tarry here below;
Why their treasures must be hidden
  From their doting eyes away,
Why for hours of transient pleasure
  They with years of pain must pay.

Why the child to us as precious
  As our own life thus should go
From us ere our love's completeness
  We could in full measure show;
Go to leave us far more lonely
  Than the bird with rifled nest,
Than the sweet girl waiting vainly
  For her whilom frequent guest.

Why the sister he so bravely
  Used to champion and defend,
Used to comfort when some trial
  Rain-like made her tears descend,
Must with their wee playmate wonder
  And so piteously cry,

THE VENTURE. 227

"Where is Cliffie? I want Cliffie,"
  As the lonely hours go by.

Why instead of warm arms twining
  Round her neck, and kisses sweet
From the pure, soft lips wont often
  "Don't cry, Bertha," to repeat,
She can only have, when troubled,
  The poor privilege to turn
And gaze on the pictured features
  Of the boy for whom we yearn.

Yet the thought that he is happy,
  And will be forevermore
Safe from sin and every evil, ·
  That makes up earth's woeful store,
Is a balm for all our heartache,
  Is a comfort for our grief,
And faith whispers, "Time is fleeting,
  Separation will be brief."

So we meekly plead, "Our Father,
  Ever wise and just and kind,
Let our child, our absent darling,
  Prove a golden tie to bind
Us to Thee and all things holy,
  Till we too with Thee may dwell,

228   *THE VENTURE.*

And in adoration lowly,
  Sing, 'Thou doest all things well.'"

TO A NEW-BORN INFANT.

Welcome, helpless little stranger,
  Welcome to our mundane sphere,
With its darkness and its danger,
  With its light, its warmth, its cheer.

Welcome to the home death rendered
  Strangely silent and forlorn,
While in chastened souls he gendered
  Sympathy for all who mourn.

Welcome, fragile little darling,
  To the hearts so sorely pained,
By one loss they scarce could notice
  Blessings manifold remained.

Welcome to their hearts all lonely,
  To that vacant crib and chair,
They have treasured, they have guarded
  With devoted zeal and care.

Welcome to their mutual fondness,
  Pride and fervent gratitude,

THE VENTURE.

Fearing, hoping, watching, praying,
　All we call solicitude.

Welcome to the wee girl, longing
　For the elder brother, who
Was to her so fondly tender,
　Sympathizing, generous, true.

Welcome to her childish wonder
　And devoted sister-love,
Which by gentle words and actions
　She delightedly will prove.

Doubly welcome, and if heaven
　Will permit thee, tarry long,
Adding to earth's store of blessing
　And its upward-pressing throng.

TO MARY ON HER WEDDING DAY.

God bless thee on thy wedding day,
　My cherished friend;
And ever through life's devious way,
　Thy steps attend.

May the deep love and trust which thrills
　Thy spirit now,

THE VENTURE.

Till all thy being freely wills
    A solemn vow,

Ne'er lose in fervor, but remain
    Deep, warm and true,
Through calm and storm and joy and pain,
    Life's journey through.

Others may offer gold and gifts,
    Of costly price
To be unto thy wedded love
    Preserving spice.

I only give a woman's love,
    A woman's prayers,
A woman's pledge to sympathize
    In all thy cares.

God bless thee! I have said the words
    In days gone by,
And say them now with quivering lip,
    And tear-moist eye.

Bless thee! and help him who has won
    Thy heart and hand,
And claims the right, close by thy side
    Henceforth to stand.

THE VENTURE. 231

To keep with true, religious care
  The solemn vow
He makes to day to cherish thee,
  Through weal and woe.

AFTER THE WEDDING.

It is ended, the solemn service,
  Which required but a little time,
And the blushing maid of the morning
  And the man in life's full prime
Are bound in so close a union
  That division would be a crime.

It is over, the mirth and feasting,
  The wishes for joy untold
Are said, and the gifts are given,
  The land, the silver and gold,
And the guests to their homes have departed,
  And the room is empty and cold.

And they, the man and the woman,
  Who yesterday were twain,
Go joyfully forth together
  To share life's pleasure or pain,
To bear an equal portion
  In each other's loss and gain.

THE VENTURE.

Go, another home to fashion,
    Another lamp to light,
Another doubled influence
    To exert for wrong or right;
Go, each to add their portion
    To earth's misery or delight.

God bless the man and the woman,
    And wherever their steps may tend
Go lovingly on before them,
    As their Guide and unfailing Friend,
And keep their love undiminished,
    · Until death shall their union end.

CPSIA information can be obtained
at www.ICGtesting.com
Printed in the USA
BVHW041229060322
630760BV00014B/717